Every president must navigate the relationship of religious faith, both public and private, to the presidency. Barack Obama did this with exceptional grace, wisdom, and skill, which will set a precedent for those who follow.

Wesley Granberg-Michaelson

Such awful treatment he received, but when you think about it, you have millions of people who now have healthcare insurance because of him. He has done what five presidents have not been able to do and that's to give universal healthcare to Americans.

Bishop Vashti Murphy McKenzie

Through his Christian faith and his faith in America, President Obama spoke eloquently to our nation for eight years in times of celebration and tragedy. I have no doubt he will be remembered as one of our greatest presidents. We will miss his leadership.

Jim Winkler

My oldest grandson was born a month before President Barack Hussein Obama was elected president of the United States. All he knows is that the president is an African-American. He has no historical perspective on how meaningful it is or how difficult it was or what his grandparents endured. He has lived his life with an African-American in the White House who had an African-American wife and two African-American daughters.

The Right Reverend Anne Henning Byfield

In the end, the lasting legacy of his presidency surely lies not just on the level of particular policy agreements, disagreements, and changes, but rather with Mr. Obama's ability as someone of a particular and clear ethnic identity to be the president of all within our nation while not in any way diminishing his own identity or diminishing the seriousness of unresolved issues relating to race.

David A. Renwick

President Obama and his administration moved the needle on the subject of immigration reform, just not far enough. It remains my single biggest disappointment about his presidency, though I suspect it is not nearly as disappointing to me as it is to him.

Dr. Felipe N. Martinez

As an African-American father, I adamantly deplore the foregoing and enduring portrayals of Black males as irresponsible, lazy, inherently violent and criminal, and highly sexual. In President Obama, my sons see a Black male father and husband, not only in their house but in the White House, who is the exact opposite of those stereotypes.

Dr. D. Darrell Griffin

Given the condition of the country that elected President Obama, I am thoroughly convinced that his enduring legacy will be extolled by the knowledge of his intense desire and determination to assure that America lived up to its constitutional mandate—in spite of all of the unfair, biased, hostile criticism that he faced, endured, and overcame for two terms.

Dr. Gerald L. Durley

One of the great legacies of the presidency of Barack Hussein Obama lies rooted in the perception of how black and brown youth can now see themselves.

Dr. Wendell Anthony

A biracial president who was bipartisan affirmed, "I've got relatives who look like Bernie Mac and I've got relatives who look like Margaret Thatcher." He bridged the racial divide of identity in his family and sought to heal the wounds of a country that he loves dearly.

Dr. Eddie Connor

Mr. Obama's legacy is secure, and his eight years as our leader have revealed that he is not only brilliant, politically savvy, and calm under enormous pressure, but that he is one who has held firm to his convictions and the ideals that make one respected, revered, and worthy of emulation.

Dr. Charles E. Booth

Mr. President

Interfaith Perspectives on the Historic Presidency of Barack H. Obama

DARRYL D. SIMS

Published by Sims Publishing Group, Washington, DC 20003
www.simspublishing group.com
Mr. President: Interfaith Perspectives on the Historic Presidency of Barack H. Obama

Library of congress Cataloging-in-Publication Data

Mr. President: Interfaith Perspectives on the Historic Presidency of Barack H. Obama
p. cm

Darryl D. Sims
ISBN 978-1-939774-30-9 (pbk. :alk. Paper)
Historical. 2. Christian Conduct. 3. Religious Life

Sims, Darryl D.

Printed in the U.S.A.
Interior layout: Delaney-Designs

DEDICATION

No person truly matures spiritually in a manner pleasing to God without the nurturing of loving and patient mentors. I dedicate this Spirit-filled book of powerful interfaith reflections to my spiritual mentor and life partner, the late Tom Skinner. His coaching and guidance helped me to become the kind of leader who could be both cheerleader and critic of President Barack Obama.

BWS

I would like to dedicate this book to the all people within the United States who have worked and continue to work for a more perfect union.

DDS

Mr. President

CONTENTS

ACKNOWLEDGEMENTS

I am especially grateful for every faith leader who took the time from challenging schedules to provide profound reflections on the historic leadership and legacy of President Barack Obama. Whether they agreed or disagreed with his policy positions, all took the time to say, "Thank you, Mr. President, for serving with such grace, style, intellect, and love for America."

BWS

I greatly appreciate Patricia McDougall for providing the photo for the cover of this book. I immensely appreciate the cover design and attentiveness received from the team of Kim, Tiffani, and Todd of Echos Media Group (Durham, NC). I thank Dr. George E. Holmes for his consistent motivation and uplift throughout the publishing process. I thank Minister Barbara Jacqueline Jeter and Minister Marteal Pitts for their endless support of this project. I wish to thank writer/editor Randy Frame, who contributed his editorial and organizational skills to this project. Most importantly, I want to thank Dr. Barbara Williams-Skinner for embracing the collective vision and helping in countless ways to make it come to pass. Collectively, they all worked together to honor unquestionably one of America's finest presidents—President Barack H. Obama.

DDS

Mr. President

PREFACE: About This Book

Contributors to this book graciously responded to the request to offer reflections on the Obama presidency. Virtually all entries could have fallen easily into the category "The Obama Legacy." But to make this resource as accessible as possible, we organized the material based on the six categories listed in the Table of Contents. To the extent that contributors focused on more than one specific aspect of the Obama legacy, some decisions on where to place their entries were highly subjective.

It should also be noted that while some contributors wrote their reflections after the election of November 8, 2016, the majority of entries came to the editors prior to that date. It's possible that some reflections would have been different—at least in tone, if not in content—had contributors known that a change in the nation's landscape was in store. Ultimately, however, the election of 2016 likely registered a negligible, if any, effect on the thoughts, perspectives, and emotions surrounding President Barack Obama's historic eight-year term.

FOREWORD ONE

HONORING THE IMAGE OF GOD
by Jim Wallis

Then God said, "Let us make humankind in our image, according to our likeness; and let them have dominion over the fish of the sea, and over the birds of the air, and over the cattle, and over all the wild animals of the earth, and over every creeping thing that creeps upon the earth." So God created humankind in his image, in the image of God he created them; male and female he created them.

This is the foundational text in Genesis 1, revealing the purpose of God in creation, the vocation of stewardship for all human beings, and the foundational value of every human being made in the image of God (*imago dei*).

This text is also the theological undermining and biblical rebuke of white supremacy. Instead of all the people made in God's image *together* having dominion (or better translated--stewardship) over the rest of creation, in America one people decided to have violent dominion over other peoples by saying they weren't fully human, thus throwing away *imago dei*.

That was America's original sin. It was not just the slavery, as there had been other slaveries before ours that didn't actively dehumanize the slave. But since white people and white Christians knew they couldn't do to indigenous people and kidnapped Africans what they were doing in taking free land, labor, and lives away from other human beings who were created in the image of God, we said they were all less than human, and even wrote that into our Constitution.

The election of Barack Obama to the Presidency of the United States was a fundamental blow to white supremacy—a black man in the highest office of the land and the most powerful position in the world. That was and will always be the greatest legacy of the Obama presidency—a historic moment in the longstanding and ongoing movement to undo white supremacy and privilege. This historic moment challenged and threatened all the ways original sin still lingers.

I remember election night in 2008. Our home hosted an election watch party with mostly twenty-somethings filling our house. Early on, Obama was expected to win; most of the young people in my house were celebrating, even out dancing in the streets of our multi-racial neighborhood.

But I was still with most of the old black guys who lived in our neighborhood—not sure I really believed that a black president would be elected in our lifetimes. If all the "undecideds" went against him in the end, Obama would lose. I was the only one left in the house watching the returns as the votes he needed for his electoral victory were officially tabulated and the election called. When that happened, I quietly and privately broke down in tears, but soon went to the streets to join the next generation who were ready to help build the bridge to a new America with the majority of minorities that will exist by 2040. We all went to Obama's inauguration with two million other people on one of the coldest January days in history. Our nation seemed ready for the new America that Barack Obama represented.

But the white backlash began almost immediately. Republican leaders announced their primary goal to make his presidency fail before it even began, even though he was trying to reach out to them. The never-ending accusations and falsehoods began, including even a conspiratorial racist campaign to prove that the new black president didn't have a birth certificate and wasn't really one of "us," i.e., a real American. (Of course, that same lie would help Donald Trump launch his political career in 2011).

A Congressman yelling, "You lie!" during the president's State of the Union speech; indignity after indignity; and continuing false claims that one of the most explicitly Christian Presidents ever (the first to do things like hosting an annual Easter breakfast in the White House) was actually a secret Muslim! I became a friend of State Senator Obama's shortly after his adult conversion to Christianity and was on President Obama's first faith-based council. We have often spoken of his personal faith and talked about how it should best shape public leadership and policy.

Some of the most hypocritical attacks have come from people on the Religious Right who claim they are for "family values," then completely ignore some of the clearest and best family role models the White House has ever seen. Obama as a husband and father, together with Michelle, has shown our nation's children some of the best demonstrations of healthy and strong family life of any U.S. President.

Take a moment and listen in your mind to all the ugly rhetoric and hateful language directed toward Barack Obama during his presidency and even in the 2016 presidential campaign. Close your eyes and listen to all the painful words you remember. I know it's hard. But then remember and declare the opening three words of the Genesis 1:26 passage above. "Then God said. . . ."

What God said is so much more important than the words of white backlash to what God has said. It is indeed God's voice that is the most powerful response to all the language of hate and fear that represents the death knell of white supremacy in this country, despite being one of the ugliest things to witness during the Presidency of Barack Obama.

Barack Obama's legacy has and will always be central to that vision of a "beloved community," as Dr. King called it, where our public and civil life is rooted in the spiritual foundation of the truth—that all of us are created in the image of God. That is the word, God's Word, that will ultimately defeat the recurring original sin of American society where privilege and punishment are based on skin color.

Barack Obama's legacy is the public refutation of that sin and a call to repentance—turning around and going in a whole new direction (always the meaning of true repentance), making our way to a new and demographically transformed America. And that is also the reason there has been such a deep racial backlash to this new America that has even now served as the underlying motivation for a presidential candidate of a major political party.

This has nothing to do with always agreeing with Obama's policies and priorities. Many religious leaders have pushed President Obama to do more to address issues of poverty, economic justice, and immigration, while some have objected to his use of drones. I have sometimes been among those offering these challenges. After public attention focused on so many police shootings of young African-American men and women, Obama more strongly stood up for racial justice in our policing and criminal justice systems. He brought health care to millions of people who had been without it. And in what may be one of his most lasting legacies, President Obama has already had significant achievements and set into place a strong direction for dealing with the urgent issue of climate change, a legacy that will benefit all of our children.

But ultimately it will be more than the impressive list of accomplishments that will determine the legacy of President Barack Obama. It will be what he has represented for the future as the first black man to win the White House and how God has used this man to help America further along the process of repenting of our original sin and building a new America.

Jim Wallis is the founder of *Sojourners* magazine and of the Washington, DC-based Sojourners community.

FOREWORD TWO

THE OBAMA PRESIDENCY:
A Prophetic Presence in the White House
by James Forbes, Jr.

What if the Obama Administration was not just another chapter in our nation's quest to become a more perfect union, but rather a providential, prophetic revelation of who we really are and what we must do if we are to become a truly democratic republic? This is more than a mere suggestive subjunctive; it is my firm conviction that what we experienced during the two terms of President Barack Hussein Obama speaks directly to the heart and soul of the psyche and spirit of America.

Citizens of the United States would be wise to consider the admonition of the song from the musical based on Alice Walker's book, *The Color Purple*: maybe God is trying to tell us something. Are we free and honest enough to listen to the poignant truth the events of the last eight years reveal to us about ourselves? A serious review of the unprecedented trials and triumphs experienced by the first African-American commander-in-chief calls us as a nation to lament, repent, and denounce, and also to appreciate, celebrate, and rededicate, our best efforts toward the restoration of respect and honor for the highest office of the land.

On November 4, 2008, my heart was flooded with pride, joy, and a measure of incredulity as the newly elected first family took the stage at Grant Park in Chicago. The opening words of President-elect Obama's victory speech brought tears to the eyes of the multi-racial gathering who knew that we were witnessing something uniquely American at its genuine best. This is what he said:

> *If there is anyone out there who still doubts that*
> *America is a place where all things are possible;*
> *who still wonders if the dream of our founders is*
> *alive in our time; who still questions the power*
> *of our democracy; tonight is your answer.*

Shortly after his inauguration, disturbing evidence began to surface, indicating that, for many, Obama could never be the answer and that every effort would be made to turn that assessment into a self-fulfilling prophecy. We have witnessed unrelenting indignities, partisan stonewalling, vilification and demonization of both the executive office and its occupant. Obvious miscalculations have been magnified exponentially; proposed compromises identified as signs of weakness; initiatives sabotaged; and then the resulting failed ventures claimed as proof of cowardice or incompetence and lack of dedication, commitment, or leadership ability.

The list goes on, but that is not the only list. During the full length of both terms, our president has earned global respect as a leader with maturity, integrity, character, competence and reliability. In every major crisis we have faced as a nation, he has functioned as negotiator-in-chief, pastor-in-chief, teacher-in-chief, healer-in-chief, and commander-in-chief. He has skillfully maximized executive authority for creative maneuvering around political obstruction and obfuscations. He has shown balanced empathy and broad sensitivity toward both sides of contentious debates. He weathered the slings and arrows of vicious attacks and, as First Lady Michelle Obama says it, when others have gone low he has modeled taking the high road. He never embarrassed this nation with personal disgrace, nor did he demonize his opponents as lacking the right to be respected as human beings. In his humility he has avoided claims of perfection, yet he has held his head high, and after tender moments of disappointment he has recovered his youthful swagger and proud self-affirmation as a man in whom the blood of white and black ancestors flows unimpeded with a steady determination to make its appointed rounds.

It is interesting that in Olympic competitions the degree of difficulty is a consideration in the score one receives. By that standard, we who have observed how well our President performed under almost impossible conditions will want to rethink and fairly judge how blessed we are to have had the Obamas in the White House during the past eight years. Even political opponents may wish to find the grace to express at least modest appreciation for a leader who did his very best to serve us and our families as we struggle to be decent and productive human beings.

As we pray to God for blessings upon our next President and Vice President, cabinet and staff, Congress and judiciary colleagues, surely we do not want to be remiss in showing gratitude for all the Obama administration means to our nation and the world. May we prove to be deserving of the quality of leadership we have experienced since 2008.

I am honored to join with my interfaith colleagues represented in this volume in giving our perspectives on the historic presidency of Barack Hussein Obama. In the midst of perplexing and inexplicable events suffused by race and class tensions, fierce ideological polarities, and rancorous and angry rhetoric, faith leaders are expected to speak to the people in response to the question: Is there a word from the Lord about the intense hostility that is spreading across our land? As I observed the bitter response to the election of President Obama, I felt the need to find an explanation for how he was able to win the election to national office given the deep rift between segments of our population. I offer the following story of my understanding of how and why he was elected and, more importantly, how we can hope to move beyond incurable group divisions toward becoming the united and not the divided states of America.

> *There is a tradition in heaven that when martyrs suffer death, a 40-year special commemoration is arranged to demonstrate that they did not shed their blood in vain. Bobby Kennedy and Martin Luther King, Jr., were both assassinated in 1968. Bobby Kennedy near the end of his life had predicted that we would have a black president in a few years, and Martin Luther King, Jr., had assured us on the eve of his assassination that we as a people will reach the promised land. They were assured by the Great Spirit that in their honor an event would take place on earth where the full value of justice and equality would have the backing of the God of the universe. A black man would become the president of the United States. On November 4, 2008, it happened according to the divine mandate.*

> *I was amazed because of my experience as the first African-American senior minister of The Riverside Church in New York City. The initial celebration that greeted my arrival easily morphed into evidence of deep misgivings as to whether all*

people are really ready for full racial inclusion. I expected that Mr. Obama would discover that, even though he had been popularly elected, he would eventually see that many were not ready to embrace the historic role he had been selected to fulfill.

My legendary account suggests that it would never have happened were it not for divine intervention. Events in our nation today confirm my suspicions. America had not suddenly become a post-racial society. We were being given the opportunity to discover how deep white supremacy is and how much work has to be done to move us into the full reality of being the land of the free and the home of the brave.

As we come to the end of two terms of a most remarkable presidency—variously characterized by some as one of the most impressive in recent history and impugned by others as totally disastrous—there is a need for in-depth analyses of what forces figured in such widely differing perspectives and assessments. Those who take time to look beneath the surface of the partisan gamesmanship or the facile dissatisfactions and disagreements rooted in disapproval of timing, style, or policy approach will find it helpful to consider the spirit of the song we've mentioned before. Maybe through the Obama experience, God is trying to tell America something about what it will take for us to become the beloved community.

Dr. James A Forbes, Jr., Pastor Emeritus of The Riverside Church of New York and Founder and President of Healing of the Nations Foundation

Mr. President

INTRODUCTION

Mr. President
by Dr. Barbara Williams-Skinner

Mr. President: Interfaith Perspectives on the Historic Presidency of Barack H. Obama

is a genius vision that God gave to fellow Howard University School of Divinity alum, Reverend Darryl Sims. The vision was for some of the most respected, dedicated, and diverse interfaith leaders across America to share reflections on the first African-American president of the United States. This was not just a great idea; it was a God idea! Who but God, who accomplishes in us "infinitely more than we might ask or think," could give America, through Barack H. Obama, a small glimpse of what our nation united might look like? Who but God could open the minds of enough Americans to twice elect a man born to a single-parent white mother and a Kenyan father? Add that his middle name, Hussein, sounded too much like some whose names we have come to fear.

Beyond all else, Sims and I shared a concern that one of the most vilified, insulted, and openly resisted American presidents would be hailed a failure in the not-too-distant future by historians and pundits. To us, failure could hardly be associated with this president. What other leader of the free world had received such a startling announcement at the start of his administration? Weeks into his presidency, Barack Obama was told by the congressional leader of the opposing political party that the party's singular goal was to make him a one-term president. What other president received such an historic level of death threats? Indeed, the greatest fear of black Americans and citizens of conscience for eight years was that he would be assassinated. And what other commander-in-chief succeeded in office despite having every proposal he offered meet with stubborn resistance, no matter how beneficial to Americans of all backgrounds? It seems there were only two questions asked by Obama detractors for nearly eight years. First: "Can anything good come out of Chicago?", the city that nurtured Obama spiritually and politically. Second: "Can anything good come out of Black America?", from a once enslaved people now heading the nation's highest office?

Mr. President is the best way for us to ensure a more balanced perspective on the impact of the Obama legacy. In it are voices of diverse faith leaders, many of them trailblazers of the Civil Rights movement, a movement that made the Obama presidency possible. Others had blazed trails in their own unique, often un-heralded, ways as spiritually inspired bridge builders and barrier breakers, seeking to model and build the Beloved Community.

Understandably, Obama's presidency evoked enormous pride among African Americans and other Americans as a hopeful sign of racial progress. Many older African Americans thought it would never happen during their lifetime. They understood that he was not the "President of Black America," but for all Americans. Yet private conversations with many black faith leaders suggested that some were downright fearful of ever op-posing him even when they thought he had not done enough for African Americans or for the poor and working poor. First, they would be attacked as an Obama hater. Second, they would give "real Obama haters" more encouragement if faith community leaders openly opposed him.

We identified dynamic faith leaders who supported President Obama on some policy positions and opposed him on others. Our task was to engage those who would speak truthfully, yet fairly, on the impact of the Obama legacy nationally and internationally. We were seeking their views on special memories that his historic presidency evoked. We wanted to hear their perception of victories, such as passage of the Affordable Care Act and his championing My Brother's Keeper to give boys of color opportunities to succeed. We also welcomed their disappointments over particular stances by the president, including his support of gay marriage, his failure to appoint an African American to the Supreme Court, his failure to advance an urban policy to address high unemployment among African-American youth. We were interested as well in perspectives on civil and human rights and whether African Americans and vulnerable citizens really benefitted from an Obama presidency.

Despite the shortness of time, we were blessed to receive dozens of profound, insightful, and thoughtful reflections expressing a full range of views on the short- and long-range impact of the Obama legacy. Our objective is to use this finished project as a means to help retain a piece of America's history and the legacy of President Barack H. Obama, and, subsequently, to provide a book that uplifts all of America's citizens. We realize it will take many years to assess the full impact of the Obama legacy on young children of color, who for eight years saw a family in the White House that looked like them. It is through their eyes, their lives, their life journeys and those of children of other races that the world will come to know the true impact and meaning of the historic presidency of Barack Hussein Obama.

On a personal note, I was among the first African-American leaders to support President Obama. His amazingly reconciling message during the 2004 Democratic Convention caused me to sit up straight in bed where I was watching the convention. What an encouragement it was for me as a bridge builder and peacemaker among people of different races and cultures to hear him say so powerfully that "there's not a liberal America and a conservative America; there's the United States of America. . . .There's not a black America and white America and Latino America and Asian America; there's the United States of America." Not since hearing Martin Luther King, Jr. speak while I was a student at University of California, Berkeley, had a messenger reached out and touched the bruised soul of a divided nation. Curious, I visited his U.S. Senate office in 2006 where he held open sessions for interested citizens on issues like education, jobs, and justice. I left my business card with his aides, never expecting to be contacted.

Three later encounters with him impressed me with the kind of visionary leader he might be. The first occurred during the 2007 election campaign. Nearly all my friends and associates endorsed Hillary Clinton. She was seen as heir apparent to the presidency. She was a former First Lady and a U.S. Senator from New York who had "stood by her man" during the Bill Clinton sex scandal and impeachment proceedings. Yet in my gut I was just not feeling Clinton, but did not really understand Senator Obama's vision for America. During the 2007 Congressional Black Caucus (CBC) Annual Legislative Conference, with Clinton being treated like a rock star, Barack Obama, a member of CBC but not well known in black political circles, was ignored.

I received a call inviting me to a gathering of potential African-American Obama supporters, probably because of my visit to his Senate office months earlier. As former director of the Congressional Black Caucus, familiar with most key black leaders, I found myself in a room with black professionals and organizational leaders who were total strangers. Prior to his arrival, there was some jockeying for who would sit closest to Senator Obama. I believed in the biblical admonition that when you enter a room filled with important people, you should "sit in the lowest seat until you are called up front." I did just that. Amazingly, when the door opened and candidate Obama walked in, he took the closest seat to the door next to me. Just before he was introduced, I asked about his plan to address poverty in America, in response to which he mentioned health care for millions of uninsured working poor Americans and a jobs proposal. That day, he became my candidate.

A second encounter with President Obama had a divine ring to it. As a member of the Circle of Protection, a network of progressive evangelical leaders protecting the poor against budget cuts, a dozen of us visited the president in 2011. Our group's mission was to get him to advocate more openly for the poor and to actually use the word "poor" when discussing the budget, something he had not done. Walking into the Roosevelt Room near the Oval Office, I looked for my nametag to take my seat, just before the president was to enter. Unbelievably, I was right in the middle of the conference table across from where President Obama sat when he entered the room. Wow!

There was much tension in the room as the mostly white clergy group introduced themselves. As I looked across the table at President Obama, suddenly I saw, through spiritual eyes, a man facing enormous decisions and a husband and father. He looked tired. So I reached across the table and asked, "Mr. President, would you mind if I prayed for you?" Without hesitation, he reached out and took my hand as I prayed for him, creating a strong spiritual connection between us for the balance of his presidency. The photo of our hands across the table in a meeting of evangelicals concerned about the poor went out far and near.

The White House particularly used it when media buzz about the president being a Muslim heated up.

A third encounter took place when the president "evolved" from supporting traditional marriage while campaigning and at the start of his presidency to embracing gay marriage in a very public announcement. I was shocked and very disappointed as one who loved all of God's children but supported traditional marriage as a matter of faith and as an exercise of my religious freedom. Though I was part of a cadre of African-American clergy who received a "heads up" on key decisions of the president, we were blindsided on this announcement. Four hours after his press conference on this game-changing pronouncement, we received a call from President Obama letting us know what he had just done and why. Some pastors said, "Mr. President, we have your back!" Speaking up, I said, "Mr. President, because you embraced traditional marriage as a candidate, I supported you and rallied evangelicals across the country in support of your presidency. As a matter of my faith understanding, I totally disagree, but will continue to work with you on issues impacting African-Americans and the poor." Waiting for his response, I thought to myself, "Well, that's the last time I'll be invited to the White House." To my relief, he said, "Barb (which no one calls me), I respect your position." The call quickly ended. Though disappointed with his position, I appreciated that we could disagree without being disagreeable.

As Barack Hussein Obama, America's 44th president, exits the White House, our nation has been exceedingly fortunate to have a decent, caring, compassionate, smart, and visionary groundbreaker. We, as a nation, must be truly grateful to have had a scandal-free White House with a strong all-American family that happened to be African American. For many years to come, we will appreciate the blessing of a great leader with strong spiritual and moral roots to help guide our Republic during times of great challenge at home and around the globe.

Dr. Barbara Williams-Skinner is President of Skinner Leadership Institute, which she co-founded in 1992. The Skinner Leadership Institute was formerly known as Tom Skinner Associates, where she was Vice President from 1981 to 1992.

Historic Moment

The Significance of the Country Choosing its First Black President

A Living Portrait of a True Family

by Rev. Dr. Otis Moss, Jr.

Mr. President, we are eternally grateful to God to have witnessed your two magnificent terms as president and commander-in-chief of our great nation. We continue to pray with you and your family as you come to the close of a history-making and history-bearing memorable moment in the life of our nation, a time when democracy lit a new candle in the dark valleys of despair and when children, adults, and the aged felt fresh winds of hope. You and the historians of the future will document the great accomplishments of the Obama era with calm reasonableness and profound analysis.

You and our wonderful First Lady Michelle Obama, along with daughters Malia and Sasha, have personified such a living portrait of true family that your opponents and detractors ceased talking about "family values." They even embraced a candidate with three wives (two divorced), a vocabulary of vulgarity, and a demeanor of disrespect, whereas your presidency has consistently pointed us to "the rising sun of a new day begun" and motivated a generation to "march on till victory is won."

You have traveled across the nation and the world etching the words of a great poet on the soul of the planet: "Come my friends, 'tis not too late to seek a newer world." You entered the White House with the courage of Joshua, the "audacity of hope," the dream of a prophet, the compassion of an apostle of love, and the passion of a disciple of justice and reconciliation. You will leave office with greater wisdom born of experience, a profound sense of service and sacrifice, and the irrevocable greatness that comes from both.

Otis Moss, Jr. is Pastor Emeritus of Olivet Institutional Baptist Church in Cleveland, Ohio

TWO HISTORIC DAYS

by His Eminence Cardinal Donald Wuerl

The election of Barack Obama as the first African-American president of the United States was itself a historic event. It marked a milestone of progress and inclusion for our country. The national significance of the event was reflected in the huge crowd, the tens of thousands of people from all over the country, who filled the streets and Capitol grounds to cheer on the president and First Lady.

As I sat on the platform for this inauguration, my thoughts went back to an earlier swearing in ceremony in 1961 of the first Catholic president. This, too, was another step along the way in our country to full inclusion. Then I was a student here in Washington in the early '60s and made my way to stand along the parade route and get as close as possible to the steps of the Capitol. Both days had several things in common. The sky was clear, the temperature was very low, the spirit of America was joyous, and history was being made.

Then we were recognizing the crossing of an anti-Catholic barrier that had been in place from the days of the arrival of Catholics in the English-speaking colonies in the early 17th century. With the election of President Obama another barrier came crashing down; this one had held back a black person from this exalted level of political life. With the reaching of both of these walls of prejudice, we came another step closer to realizing the dream of Dr. Martin Luther King, Jr.: "To speed up that day when all of God's children, black men and white men, Jews and Gentiles, Protestants and Catholics, will be able to join hands..."

The parallels between these two recognized leaders are real. The grandfather of John Fitzgerald Kennedy would have seen signs as a young man in his part of the country, "Irish need not apply." The generation just prior to Barack Obama would have been greeted with signs, "Blacks to the back of the bus."

As President Obama completes his term of office, we can all praise God that we live in a land where we proclaim and try to live: "We hold these truths to be self-evident, that all men are created equal." History also tells us that between the saying and the doing, between the words and the reality, there is always the need for faith, perseverance, determination, commitment, and compassionate understanding. We have all just witnessed another great step forward in what it takes to realize those words more fully.

As I listened to President Obama take the oath of office, I could not help but rejoice in the blessings of liberty that are so much the heritage of our nation. Sometimes those blessings require a struggle to achieve but they are nonetheless present. With the grace of God and the good will of the people of our country, all of us in America have moved forward one more giant step. One cannot help but sense the reality of the power of amazing grace.

His Eminence Cardinal Donald Wuerl is Archbishop of Washington, DC and serves as an American prelate of the Catholic Church. He is the sixth Archbishop of Washington, serving since 2006.

Mr. President

A WORD OF THANKS TO PRESIDENT BARACK H. OBAMA
by Bishop George Battle

President Barack H. Obama
The White House
Washington, D.C.

I am honored and deeply grateful to have this opportunity to extend my thoughts and personal thanks to you for all the work you have done as the 44th president of the United States of America. Words fail me in my attempt to properly convey all that I feel for you, our country, and the African-American communities. It is with great honor that I congratulate you on being elected to the presidency of the United States of America. Your integrity and humility speak well of you. Your ability to maintain the "high road" in the midst of countless attacks and character assassinations has been a model for us all. Without doubt, you are an inspirational leader who displays not only charming charisma but also Christian character.

If there is anyone out there who doubts that America is a place where anything is possible, who still wonders if the dream of our founders is alive in our time, who still questions the power of our democracy, Mr. President, that night of November 4, 2008 changed the face of history for all Americans, particularly African-Americans. The moment encapsulated all the hopes and dreams of the African-American people. For hundreds of years, stories of African kings and queens, enslaved ancestors, and the civil rights movement have been the backdrop for lessons of encouragement and achievement. While it is those stories that are dear to my heart and still encourage me as the Senior Bishop of the A.M.E. Zion Church to press forward, today's society was in need of something more tangible—a more current reality to compel them to greatness. The election of the 44th president of the United States of America, Barack Hussein Obama, has given us a fresh yet tangible story to encourage our people to excellence.

The transition in the White House not only reinstituted the thought of hope and set a standard for excellence, but it also demonstrated transference of power. The national government, until now, has been retained and prominently controlled by Caucasians only; therefore, power was associated with skin color. The transformation of power was a wonderful scriptural illustration of the Ephesians 3:20 power: **"Now to him who is able to do exceedingly above all that we ask or think, according to the power that works in us."**

You stand not only in the tradition of your 43 predecessors who have assumed this high office before you, but you stand in the tradition of the judges and kings of the Old Testament, many of whom were even younger than you when they assumed their leadership responsibilities. It is in the spirit of those traditions –most especially the Davidic tradition—that I salute you as our president.

Mr. President, I believe the hand of the Lord was upon you for such a time as this. I believe you have been given this moment in history to show forth the glory of Almighty God.

Bishop George Edward Battle, Jr. is Senior Bishop of the African Methodist Episcopal Zion Church and Presiding Prelate of the Piedmont Episcopal District.

BLACK MILLENNIALS, BLACK CHURCH & THE OBAMA ADMINISTRATION:

Reflections from a New York City Young Adult Pastor

by Minister Gabby Cudjoe Wilkes

When President Barack Hussein Obama was elected in 2008, I was a 23-year-old, unmarried New York University graduate student living in Harlem, New York City. The night he was elected, I took to the streets with my roommate, where we and the rest of Harlem danced the electric slide, hugged strangers, and had an all-out dance party in the streets of Harlem. It was midnight and we were all beaming with joy and pride. We simply could not believe that a black man had actually been elected the 44th President of the United States of America!

In 2012 when President Obama was elected for his second term, I had been married for two years, was working in entertainment publicity, and was shocked that he had done it again. We, like thousands of other Americans, drove to Washington DC for the inauguration of his second term. Now, in 2016 as his final term concludes, I am a second-year Yale University Divinity School seminarian, a licensed minister, and a millennial pastoring other millennials. There has been a black family in the White House for the bulk of my twenties. I have no doubt that this reality has shaped my worldview in ways I cannot even name. It shapes the lives of those I pastor as well.

As a New York City faith leader, I work with individuals who are hypercritical of politics and politicians, blackness, activism, and more. It isn't lost on this generation that under the Obama administration, a Nobel Peace Prize was awarded to him and yet the Black Lives Matter movement was birthed as a response to racial injustice. The Affordable Care Act was passed and yet unemployment is still in high numbers, making it challenging for millennials to find jobs. As a result, many black millennials have become entrepreneurs, unintentionally launching a resurgence of the Black Renaissance redesigned for the 21st century.

The Obama administration has forced the church to dive into traditionally taboo topics such as marriage equality, immigration rights, abortion rights, and more. As a black Christian family, the Obamas have provided an opportunity for churches to have honest dialogue about taboo issues that black churches often didn't deal with publicly. It begs the question, "What does it mean to speak truth to power, even when the highest office in our nation is held by someone who looks like 'us'?"

Perhaps the greatest gift this family has granted the black church is the understanding that African-Americans are not monolithic. We as a people hold diverse thoughts about life's most challenging issues. I would argue that the greatest gift they have offered the black community is that representation matters, yet we still must organize and advocate for justice if we want this nation to continue to evolve. I thank God for Barack Hussein Obama. His willingness to be first has changed the American narrative. May God bless and keep him for his sacrifice. The work continues.

Minister Gabby Cudjoe Wilkes serves at The Greater Allen A.M.E. Cathedral of New York.

Mr. President

THE OBAMA PRESIDENCY AND US
by Dr. Alton B. Pollard, III

I moved to Washington, DC in the fall of 2007 to begin my new assignment as dean of Howard University School of Divinity. A new presidential cycle was in full swing, and the political parties were fielding their respective candidates. Barack Obama, the junior senator from Illinois, was still a relative unknown to most rank-and-file citizens. Despite his two best-selling books and his unforgettable 2004 DNC keynote address, even Americans of African descent were hard pressed to believe that the leader of the nation would be elected from among their ranks. On January 20, 2009, the impossible happened. Barack Hussein Obama was sworn in as the 44th President of the United States.

Those were heady days—to live in the nation's capital and to work inside the beltway at the dawn of the age of Obama. I remembered an article I had written for *U.S. News and World Report*, sharing my views on the historic election of a Black president. Early in 2008, then-presidential hopeful Obama had captured the imagination of the American public with one sentence: "We are the ones we've been waiting for."

Everything draws on what has come before. Obama's words derive from a 1980 poem written by June Jordan in honor of the women of South Africa and their democratic struggle for freedom. The elders of the Hopi Nation would soon prophesy these same words. Alice Walker translated Jordan's refrain into exquisite prose. Visionaries, a multiethnic hip-hop group, captured the verse in song. Sweet Honey in the Rock turned the poet's lyrics into a choral anthem. Will.i.am made them a YouTube sensation. Barack Obama transformed them into a swelling crescendo of hope. What was originally a mantra of freedom to women had become a hymn for all people yearning to breathe free.

Nearly eight years have passed. We are approaching the end of the Obama presidency. For a time, our twice-elected president was heralded as mythic proof that ours is a common citizenry modeling a democratic society and a post-racial, post-sectarian and post-modern world. All the while, all manner of what divides us was being adroitly and selectively downplayed. No matter. Bitter enmities still flourish in issues of race, religion, nation, ethnicity, gender, social class, language, sexuality, ability, and more.

So often overlooked in our critiques of the legacy of the 44th president, for good and for ill, is one simple word: *"we."* Separateness was never the message of Obama's campaign refrain, and yet we have made of it a virtue. We the People, *E pluribus unum*, out of many one, with liberty and justice for all-- these proclamations are realized only when we actively and collectively commit to democratic freedoms. Still, there are those who seek to exploit our societal unrest and to halt the creation of a common life that is inclusive of all and alienating of none. Almost in spite of ourselves, the United States of America has become a global village—multiethnic, multicultural, multilingual, ecumenical, interfaith, intergenerational, gender diverse, creative, enterprising, flawed, and beautifully human. President Barack Obama and the first family have contributed much to our common inheritance. This uncommon moment is ours to embrace. Can we do it? *Si se puede!* Yes, we can.

Dr. Alton B. Pollard, III is Dean and Professor of Religion and Culture at Howard University School of Divinity in Washington, DC.

A DREAM COME TRUE
by Dr. Henry Davis

The presidency of Barack Obama was a dream come true to many and a surprise to others. Living and pastoring right outside of Washington, D.C. during this historical moment was extremely interesting and empowering at the same time. Early on, I began to encourage our parishioners to take seriously the candidacy of this virtual upstart, although many were supporting the candidacy of Hillary Clinton.

Prince George's County, Maryland is a unique community as it is the wealthiest African-American majority county in the United States, a dynamic that has helped us to be the home of a number of megachurch congregations. I have an uncle who has referred to it as "The Gold Coast", stating how exciting a place it is for African-Americans to reside. I heard this while pastoring in Harlem, New York before receiving the call to come pastor the First Baptist Church of Highland Park in Landover, Maryland, where our church is on the same street as FedEx Field, the home of Washington D.C.'s professional football team. If there was a community that should be excited about Barack Obama's candidacy, I really felt that ours should be it. Many in our county had been blessed to obtain degrees and have heard that if you worked hard, certain positives would come your way.

When I was working on my doctoral degree, I had the opportunity to study under Dr. Jeremiah A. Wright Jr., the pastor of the Trinity United Church of Christ in Chicago, the church Barack Obama called home. Due to my relationship with Dr. Wright, I had the opportunity to meet then-Senator Obama. I had a sense of pride to see a man of color running for the highest office in the land, and I planned to give him as much support as possible.

For years comedians joked about what would happen with a Black man in the White House (though some said that Bill Clinton would be as Black as it could get at 1600 Pennsylvania Ave.). The jokes would abound—from the food offerings to what music performers would be invited to share. And what does the new president do once he gets to the White House? He builds a basketball court out back.

African-Americans can be proud of the many accomplishments during the Obama years. We can also say that his years were absent of scandal and the kind of behavior that would make persons shrink when his name is mentioned. I was there on that cold morning when he took the oath of office as my daughter, now a second-year law student at Columbia University, and I got up early to take mass transit so that we could witness that historical moment. It was so cold that day that I couldn't even feel my feet. But I would not have missed it for the world.

Dr. Henry Davis serves as the senior pastor of First Baptist Church of Highland Park in Landover, Maryland.

HISTORIC PRESIDENCY
by Bishop Donald Hilliard

I remember it distinctly, almost like it was yesterday. It was a very cold, blustery day, among the coldest of that year. Despite the weather, the inauguration festivities of the first African-American president of the United States of America were underway. I had been fortunate enough through friends and colleagues to be invited to various celebratory inaugural balls and a few other corporate events celebrating this monumental moment. I was intentional in ensuring that I shared this prestigious, historic occasion with my wife and our three daughters. It was a momentous occasion!

My family and I bunkered down in the home of a relative. And on the day of the inauguration it was so cold that my wife and I and two of our daughters stayed in the corporate office of a friend, just a mile or so away from the actual event. My eldest daughter, Leah, and her friends would walk all the way to the inauguration to be there in person. The rest of us watched it with tears streaming down our faces as Barack Obama took the oath of office to be the president of the United States of America. What came to my mind was the poem that the late, great Maya Angelou recited when she spoke for President Bill Clinton: "The Pulse of Morning." She concluded that poem by saying, "Good morning!" It was indeed a good morning for America; a new day had dawned. We truly have come over a way that with tears has been watered. We have come treading the path through the blood of the slaughtered. Out of the dreary past, now we stand at last, where the bright dream of our hope was cast. And so we began what would be eight years of greatness, eight years of courageous, monumental leadership!

Our president had inherited one of the most disastrous seasons of our nation. And yet I believe that by divine providence God used him to turn so many things around. The least of the turnarounds would be the bailout of Chrysler, pulling us out of a recession, and bringing an end to the rule of Osama bin Laden. Of course, we have never, ever, ever heard of someone on the floor of the House call any sitting president of the United States "a liar"; but this presidency was different. This man was Black; the Senator who spoke was a white southerner who loudly and boldly yelled, "You lie!" It seems as if it was the beginning of a happy time where we were going to finally see a day when people were not judged by the color of their skin, but by the content of their character. But sad to say, there were those who just could not get with it. They could not understand, they could not yield, they could not comprehend or receive the direction and leadership of an African-American man. Nevertheless, I do believe that the Lord was with him then, and the Lord is with him now. To be sure, some of his policies and stances were far, far to the left of where I may be, but it did not undermine the effectiveness and the overall light that he brought to a very dark time.

I was proud as my daughters witnessed this event, as they had previously witnessed the inauguration of President Clinton. I was proud as a father of daughters to see President Obama's two daughters rise to the occasion. I have also watched with great pride the grace and dignity of their grandmother, Mrs. Marion Robinson, yes, the "Big Momma" of the family, living in the White House with her unashamedly African-American daughter in a house built by slaves. What a sight to witness and a legacy to behold!

And so for the last eight years we celebrated triumphs and defeats. There were those from the very beginning who determined that President Obama was not going to succeed, but succeed he has! He has done it; he has finished his course in this capacity; he has kept the faith. While laws and policies can be modified and changed, I am confident that his legacy cannot be erased. President Obama's portrait will hang in the White House rotunda in perpetuity, for while policies may be changed, history cannot be changed. An African-American man led this nation built up by slaves; we have come a long way. Yes, much needs to be done. Yes, poverty exists. Yes, there is still discrimination. But let us look on the bright side. As the old hymnologist wrote, *"There is a bright side somewhere, there is a bright side somewhere. Don't you stop until you find it. There is a bright side somewhere."*

I am grateful that I, my late mother, and my family and friends lived to see that bright side somewhere. These past eight years we have watched; our souls now, as he goes out of office, will look back and wonder, time eternal, how we got over!

Finally, I commend my dear friend for over 30 years, the Rev. Dr. Barbara Williams Skinner, for this monumental work that she has helped put together—this compilation of experiences that highlights this brilliant light that will shine forever.

Bishop Donald Hilliard, Jr., D. Min., is senior pastor at Cathedral International in Perth Amboy, New Jersey.

BEYOND MENTAL SLAVERY

by James A. Forbes, III

As a child, I remember being in school and having to recite the Pledge of Allegiance along with the entire class. I also recall a conversation that took place not long after reciting the Pledge of Allegiance where all of us were asked what we wanted to be when we grew up. The responses varied from person to person, and it seemed the answers were repeated a few times as each classmate chimed in.

I returned home that day and found myself in the same conversation with friends in our neighborhood on a playground in the center of an apartment complex not far from where I lived. The same question rang out: "What do you want to be when you grow up?" In this setting, the answers were broader than the usual: fireman, policeman, doctor, lawyer. Other vocations were voiced such as barber, milkman, convenience store manager, sanitation worker, building superintendent, subway conductor, taxi driver. These are the professions we would encounter on a daily basis, so they seemed exciting to us, something to aspire to be in the future. During this exchange on the playground I noticed that no one mentioned wanting to be a mayor, governor, congressman, congresswoman, borough president or president of the United States of America, so I decided to bring this up in class after the Pledge of Allegiance had been recited for the day. I waited for the question to come my way as I sat on the edge of my seat as if someone had spilled water on the seat and I could only wipe off the front portion. My feet were at 1:00 and 7:00, so I was ready to spring out of my chair as if I felt my pants were wet from sitting back too far in a water-soaked chair.

Finally, it was my turn, and I blurted out, "I want to be the mayor of New York!" It exclaimed it with pride and a confidence that could not be shaken, along with a huge smile on my face. The class chuckled, and the teacher instructed me gently to sit down, which puzzled me because in all my excitement to answer the question I did not realize that I had jumped out of my seat and happened to be standing up. So I took my seat, and the question continued around the classroom. As the class settled down, a classmate leaned over and said, "That was funny, James, the way you jumped out of your seat and said you wanted to be the mayor of New York." I smiled and replied, "I didn't know that I wasn't in my seat until the teacher said to sit down."

On the playground after school, I decided to tell some of my friends about my day in school. I started by telling them that when asked about what I wanted to be when I grew up, my answer was "the mayor of New York." My friends responded by laughing hysterically for almost a full minute, it seemed. I smiled and chuckled with them. Then one of my friends from the neighborhood who was older by four years said, "Ain't nobody gonna vote for a black man to be mayor, governor, or president in our lifetime; you can forget that." Everyone else chimed in, echoing the same sentiment.

The nationalities of this group ranged from Latino to African-American to Asian. The group in school was Caucasian outside of two African-Americans, me being the third. I soon realized that the laughter from my classmates and my friends in the neighborhood didn't have anything to do with my delivery. It had everything to do with WHAT I'd delivered. In their minds, what I said should have been postmarked "Return to Sender," because the contents had been sent to the wrong circulatory consciousness.

In 1984, Jesse L. Jackson sought the Democratic nomination for president. In 1988 he ran again, and I remember certain class-mates saying, "The only reason you want him to win is because he is black." I didn't give a verbal response. Instead I smiled and walked away, feeling like a small victory had been won.

In 2007, I started hearing discussions about a senator from Chicago who apparently had gained some momentum and popu-larity through the primaries. I watched this process and noticed that the general opinion was that this senator wouldn't make it through the impending primaries and would eventually drop out of the race. I listened to different political analysts critique his credentials and preparedness to run for this esteemed office. Some said it was a joke for anyone to believe he could achieve his apparent goal. Later we were led to believe that he wasn't an American citizen due to his father being from Africa as well as being Muslim. Constant focus on seeing his birth certificate flooded the airwaves as if somehow, he had been able to evade detection of his true nationality. With every new piece of nega-tive information about this senator from Chicago who dared to run for the presidency of the United States of America, I was reminded of the mental slavery that exists in our communities, slavery that says we shouldn't attempt to be anything other than normal and that extraordinary shouldn't even be a thought in our minds.

In 2008, Barack Hussein Obama successfully won the general election against Republican nominee John McCain, an event that was epic but at the same time left most of us questioning how it happened. Remember, the general consensus was that no black man would ever dawn the doors of the White House as president. On January 20, 2009 Barack Hussein Obama was inaugurated as the 44th President of the United States, and it seemed that this was the focus all over the world. It was official, notwithstanding that, as he was taking the oath, the justice who swore him in conveniently jumbled up a few lines that Senator Obama corrected on the spot, which demanded that they repeat the whole thing again after the official ceremony so that his inauguration would be official and above question.

President Obama's two terms as president have afforded him extraordinary success in the face of unprecedented opposition, as well as some extreme challenges that seemed to create an even deeper racial divide. But he didn't give up. Somewhere along this path he may have been able to hear the conversations that took place in that classroom I was a part of or on the playground in my neighborhood, where it was crazy to dare to be extraordinary. If he heard those conversations, I'm glad he ignored them along with the other naysayers who proclaimed he wouldn't and couldn't win the general election.

By ignoring those things I believe that God's light is showing us where we are, where we are headed, and where we need to be. We are still very divided, displaced as a country that should be standing together. It has been proven that we are stronger together. If we continue down the path that we are on currently, it will continue to be difficult to quote the Pledge of Allegiance with truthful hearts that we are "one nation, under God, indivisible, with liberty and justice for all." We need healing as a nation. I firmly believe that the portion of Scripture that says, "If my people, which are called by my name, will humble themselves and pray, seek my face, turn from their wicked ways, then will I hear from heaven, forgive their sin, and heal the land."

Rev. James A. Forbes III, Healing of The Nations Foundation

TRANSFORMATIONAL IMPACT
by Bishop Claude Alexander

In the Spring of 2004, I received a call from my brother concerning a fundraiser that he was holding in New York. He told me that he needed me to write a check to support an Illinois state senator named Barack Obama, who was running for the US Senate. Having been in the Chicago area during the time of the Illinois state primary, I was vaguely familiar with State Senator Obama. I gladly wrote the check to support my brother's efforts as a budding fundraiser, who would eventually raise significant amounts of money for the senatorial and first presidential campaigns. My brother was an early adopter who believed that that little-known state senator could take it all the way to the White House. He was correct. Unfortunately, my brother did not live to see the full manifestation of his belief and investment; he died in May of 2012.

When I think about the legacy of the presidency of Barack Obama, I immediately think of how the mere idea of him caused my brother to dream, to imagine a profound possibility and to give of himself and of his resources towards its realization and achievement. Whether realistic or not, Barack Obama became the object upon which the hopes and dreams of so many were deposited and the conduit through which they were energized to express themselves in the political process.

I think not only about how the idea of Barack Obama's candidacy inspired my brother to dream, but I also think about how the reality of his presidency has impacted my daughters, who are 16 and 13. The only president they have known is President Barack Obama. They have no concept of the doubts that a person of color could ever become president. Their concept has been shaped by the reality of his presidency. Such is the case for their generation. We cannot begin to imagine how transformative that reality will be for them as they mature. We do know, however, that they have had an image of a smart, disciplined, well-spoken, and focused man who has loved and honored his wife and daughters and has served his country in a way that helped elevate the place of the United States in the world. For them and for us, we can't settle for anything less.

For me, the presidency of Barack Obama in both its idea and its reality can be summed up in one word: transformational. The extent of its impact will only be told by the generations to come.

Bishop Claude Alexander serves as the senior pastor of The Park Church in Charlotte, NC.

THE SUBSTANCE OF THINGS HOPED FOR

by Dr. Gina Stewart

"Now faith is the substance of things hoped for, the evidence of things not seen." (Hebrews 11:1)

On January 20, 2009, I stood in the crowd of more than a million people in freezing temperatures to watch a junior senator from Chicago, Barack Hussein Obama, as he was sworn in as the 44th president of the United States of America. President Barack Obama, the product of an interracial relationship, became the nation's 44th president the day following the national holiday honoring Dr. Martin Luther King, Jr. On that chilly Tuesday morning in Washington, D.C., the nation and world witnessed an unprecedented moment in American history as President Obama broke the ultimate racial barrier to become the first African-American to claim the country's highest office.

President Obama was born just six years after the Montgomery bus boycott and three months after the first launch of the Freedom Riders protest of segregation. Less than 50 years before his inauguration, blacks were fighting Jim Crow discrimination, voter disenfranchisement, and legalized segregation. When President Obama and his family walked out to accept the presidency of the United States before a jubilant sea of people of every hue and nationality, his very step forward seemed to represent a giant leap toward racial progress in America. It seemed that a dream deferred was now a dream fulfilled.

On Tuesday, January 20, 2009, this nation, with its deep-seated history of slavery and racism, generations of racial strife, lynching, segregation, and oppression, witnessed a genuinely transformational moment as we saw the embodiment of this nation's highest ideals. As Coretta Scott King once remarked about the March on Washington, it appeared that, for a moment, the Kingdom appeared. Laughter, smiles, goodwill, hugs, and tears permeated the atmosphere, and I was elated to witness such an historic moment. It seemed that "our time for change had come."

And in many ways, change did come. We have witnessed many changes under an Obama administration, including but not limited to the capture of Osama Bin Laden, universal healthcare, a revived economy, increased infrastructure spending, improved conditions for women, the improvement of America's reputation around the world, the rejuvenation of the auto industry, an effort to normalize relations with Cuba, consumer protection for credit card users, tax credits for first-time homeowners, legislation to hold Wall Street accountable, the fair sentencing act, reduced disparity between crack and cocaine sentencing, and so much more. His accomplishments are legendary. Only time and eternity will reveal the complete record of his stewardship as a leader, husband, father, and public servant.

But change hasn't come easy. Since President Obama assumed the office of president, we have also witnessed partisan obstruction, blatant disrespect, demands for a birth certificate to prove his citizenship, fear mongering, increased violence, an escalation in hate crime and hate groups, numerous unnecessary and tragic shootings of unarmed men and women of color, mass incarceration, militarized police zones, obstinate resistance to gun control legislation, and racism, which remains a stain on America's soul.

As we are nearing the end of two terms with our first Black president, we are not necessarily more safe, free or equal. The Black Lives Matter movement was birthed under Obama's presidency. The school-to-prison pipeline is a disturbing national trend, and African-Americans are still 13 times poorer than our white counterparts. Perhaps this is why "faith is the substance of things hoped for, the evidence of things not seen." Thank you, President Obama. Because of your leadership, I have the audacity to hope and remain hopeful.

Dr. Gina Stewart is the senior pastor of Christ Missionary Baptist Church in Memphis, TN.

THE SERENDIPITY OF THE OBAMA PRESIDENCY

by Pastor Tyrone P. Jones IV

As President Barack Obama comes to the close of his historic two terms in office, I marvel at the fact of his meteoric rise, from his time in the Illinois State House to his failed candidacy for the United States House of Representatives to his one term as a United States senator all the way to the White House. Many even reflect on his 2004 speech at the Democratic National Convention as to what catapulted him to the White House. But to me Barack Obama did not have enough shoe leather on the ground of the political landscape to ascend to the White House with just one speech. If one speech alone could convince millions to vote for a Black man, then what happened to Rev. Jesse Jackson, Rev. Al Sharpton, Dr. Ben Carson and the Herman Cains of the world who have had similar platforms that did not lead to the presidency?

As I reflect on just how President Barack Obama got to 1600 Pennsylvania Ave., the word "serendipitous" comes to mind. Serendipity is an aptitude for making desirable discoveries by accident. Another definition refers to the highly unlikely nature of something happening that has happened. There is a serendipity to the Obama presidency.

A fairy tale called the "Three Princes of Serendip" is, I believe, apropos in describing the Obama presidency. This fairy tale is the English version of the Italian story *Peregrinaggio di tre giovani figliuoli del re di Serenddippo*, published by Michele Tramezzino of Venice in 1557. The story is about three princes who are sent on multiple journeys by their father, who felt that his sons had led sheltered lives. So he sent them off to become educated by great tutors. The tutors reported back to the king the excellent progress the princes had made in the study of arts and sciences. But the king was unsure about leaving his throne to his sons. The princes possessed great wisdom, but their father feared that their education and privilege might have caused them to live detached lives. So on one occasion, the king sent them on a trip abroad, and upon their arrival they noticed clues of a missing camel that they had never seen before. They concluded that the camel was lame, blind in one eye, missing a tooth, carrying a pregnant woman, and carrying honey and butter on its hump. They took their findings to the emperor of the distant land, and immediately the emperor accused them of stealing the lost camel. However, the three princes carefully and methodically gave specific clues and details that were derived from their close observation of the facts. Just as the emperor was about to pronounce judgment on the three princes, a traveler came in with the missing camel. The princes' lives were spared, and they were given great gifts and appointed as advisors to the emperor of the distant land. This story's English version is the source of the word "serendipity."

What does this have to do with the Obama presidency, you ask? I believe that although it was always highly unlikely for a Black man to become president, President Obama was poised, positioned, and primed to lift up what America currently is and the promise of what America is supposed to look like. In the story, President Obama does not resemble the princes' journey or their rise to power, but the duality of the Obama presidency is the visibility of the missing camel and the stranger who gets no credit but brings the camel to emperor. America has found her missing camel. The presidency of Barack Obama is a stark reminder that we do not live a post-racial society; the fact is that a gaping racial, economic, and societal wound is still open in America. The clues are ever present before us. No other president has endured what President Obama has endured. The clues are ever before us. The visibility of the vitriolic, vulgar, and violent nature of this country is a reminder of the wounded camel that was missing and is now discovered in the light of the Obama presidency. The clues are ever before us!

President Obama is also a reminder of the unknown traveler who comes in before us and brings to the forefront what was never noticed and seldom acknowledged. The unknown traveler comes and delivers but is not recognized for his accomplishments. Now that President Obama is about to leave office, his accomplishments will be scourged and scrutinized as minimal in the history of reductionist rhetoric. There was the need for the almost accidental ascension of a Barack Obama to remind us of the polar opposite to equality, harmony, and justice that lurks on the fringe of true hope and change in America.

There are many examples in the Bible of how God uses highly unlikely people to bring attention to what was missing and least discovered. It says in Matthew 19:26, "Jesus looked at them and said, 'With man this is impossible, but with God all things are possible.'" I want to conclude by stating that we can never leave out the God factor in anything that seems improbable, impossible, inconceivable, and unimaginable. My grandparents did not live to see a Black president, but they prayed that the impossible would become possible. We may not see the likes of Barack Obama any time soon, but history will record and the story will be told that eight years into the turn of the 21st century the 44th president of the United States was a Black Man.

Rev. Tyrone P. Jones IV serves as the senior pastor of First Baptist Church of Guilford in Columbia, Maryland.

SHATTERING THE ILLUSIONS OF SECOND CLASS CITIZENSHIP
by Rev. Traci Blackmon

I love the biblical story of the Exodus for both its literal and its psychological representations of liberation. I am intrigued by God's choice of Moses as deliverer because, although Moses is raised and socialized among the privileged of Egypt, Moses is Hebrew. The fact that God chooses one of their own to lead the Israelites out of bondage represents not only a physical change in their existence, but a psychological shift in their perceived possibilities. The leadership of Moses shattered illusions of second class citizenship under God.

I am not suggesting that President Barack Obama is a modern-day Moses. Nor am I suggesting that black people have received the systemic liberation needed for true equality in a nation infected with the toxicities of white supremacy and institutionalized racism. The presidency of Barack Obama has not eradicated any of the aforementioned toxic strongholds, but his presidency has shattered illusions of second class citizenship for people of color in a nation that still struggles with equality for all.

In the face of calculated political opposition to both his proposed policies and his presidency, President Obama remains an untarnished contradiction to the deeply held convictions of this nation that to be born black is to be born less than equal. Even as racist leaders questioned his authority to lead, he ignored the racist vitriol and served this nation with unbridled excellence. With strong and decisive leadership, he rescued this nation from the brink of economic disaster by signing The American Recovery and Reinvestment Act. He offered a viable solution to a widening gap in health disparities with The Affordable Care Act. He affirmed the rights of everyone to legally marry whom they choose and the rights of women to make their own reproductive decisions.

I do not agree with every position he took, and there remains much work to do. Throughout U.S. history there have been leaders who have emerged to shatter illusions of white supremacy. President Obama is such a leader for me. He stands in the lineage of those who have helped to make this nation great and to make the dreams of every American possible.

Because of Barrack Hussein Obama, we now have an entire generation of young people for whom a black president in the White House is their only reality. The wonderment of a young black boy touching the hair of the president and the pride I felt as the First Family moved in to the house built by slaves whose descendants were never intended to live there are reminders to me that those created in the image of God can never be lessened by the actions of humanity.

No matter the challenges we continue to face, when asked, "Can we overcome?", the answer will always be, "Yes, We Can!"

Rev. Traci D. Blackmon serves as Executive Minister of Justice & Witness for The United Church of Christ.

OUR CHILDREN SAW AN AFRICAN-AMERICAN PRESIDENT

by The Right Reverend Anne Henning Byfield

My oldest grandson was born a month before President Barack Hussein Obama was elected president of the United States. All he knows is that the president is an African-American. He has no historical perspective on how meaningful it is or how difficult it was or what his grandparents endured. He has lived his life with an African-American in the White House who had an African-American wife and two African-American daughters.

My grandson has pictures of President Obama in his room, and when you ask, "Who is the president?", he says, "President Obama." The admiration of an eight-year-old may seem inconsequential in light of the president's many accomplishments over the last eight years, but the election of our first African-American president has had a major positive impact on the psyche of our children and even on us.

It is the re-election of an African-American that I admire above all of the successes of the president. Twice the country said he was the leader to trust and support. He has won many victories, accomplished many goals, changed the direction of the nation in many areas, and is highly respected by political leaders around the world. He has also disappointed and frustrated others by not following what many felt was the African-American agenda. At times the African-American community felt abandoned; at times we did not like his positions; and at times we disliked him but he was still our president.

What we thought in the African-American community would never happen did happen—twice. He is an intellectual and a politically savvy spiritual leader who demonstrated a deep love for the country and humanity while showing a visible love and respect for his wife and children. There was a sheer joy in knowing that our ancestral cries and prayers had been answered.

We saw pictures of children in awe of our president touching his hair, jumping in his arms, and playing with him. I was at Rev. Dr. Clemente Pinckney's funeral, one of the martyred Charleston Nine. At the end of the service, Rev. Pinckney's daughter stood with her arms outstretched, reaching for the president to pick her up. He did, and she laid on his shoulder. One could argue that she didn't care whether he was black or white, only that he was the president. I would disagree. I had seen her interaction for a couple of days and am clear that it was a black male president who reminded her of her father from whom she sought comfort.

My grandson, while still facing racism in deplorable ways, now has one hurdle conquered for him. He sees an African-American president as the highest elected official of the land as a norm. He did not see the struggle or the attacks; he just knows it's a reality. Even in the most racist climate in years, President Obama reminds us that dreams can come true. That's a lasting reality for which I am grateful.

The Right Reverend Anne Henning Byfield is Presiding Bishop for the 16th Episcopal District of the African Methodist Episcopal Church.

AN EPOCH EVENT

by Marvin A. McMickle, Ph.D.

Over the course of American history there have been a few presidential elections that could rightfully be referred to as historic, perhaps even history-altering. The first, of course, would be the election of George Washington, the nation's first president. His election in 1789 was the definitive move away from a monarchy that was passed on within a royal family to a democratic form of government where power to select leaders resided with the people who cast their votes. Just as important was the fact that at the end of two terms he relinquished the office of the presidency, thus establishing the policy of the peaceful transfer of power. Of course, in the days of George Washington the voters were limited to white males over the age of 21 who owned 100 acres of land or more. Add to that the fact that George Washington was a slaveholder and his role in our nation's history becomes marred.

Another presidential election that was of great historic consequence was the election of Abraham Lincoln in 1860. From the moment he took the oath of office, the calls for slaveholding states to secede from the Union were already being heard. Lincoln was sworn in on March 4, 1861. Confederate forces in South Carolina fired on Fort Sumter on April 12, 1861 and the bloody Civil War began. Over time, what began as a war to preserve the Union evolved into a war to abolish slavery. As symbolic as the Emancipation Proclamation was, it did not have the immediate effect of freeing many slaves, since most slaves lived in areas that did not honor Lincoln's authority. Instead, it was the Union army and Lincoln's role in gaining passage of the Thirteenth Amendment to the U.S. Constitution that put the final nail in the coffin of slavery.

That brings us to the third history-making election, which was the election of Barack Obama in 2008. What makes his election an epoch event was all he represents about America's original sin of slavery. It would have been unimaginable to Washington or Lincoln or any other American president that any person of African ancestry who bears the conspicuous mark of non-white skin could ever become the president of the United States. The battles that were fought that led up to that moment were bloody and costly. For more than 100 years the right to vote that African Americans gained with the Fifteenth Amendment was blocked by the grandfather clause, the literacy test, the poll tax, and the lynching tree. The battle to regain the right to vote came with the Voting Rights Act of 1965, but that struggle was also stained with the blood of martyrs—Jimmy Lee Jackson, Viola Liuzzo, and James Reeb, just to name a few.

The presence of a black family in the White House, not as servants but as America's first family, was something that I never dreamed I would live to see. It is also something that many white people in America have been working very hard never to see happen again. Between the anti-Obama congressional leaders, the aggressive voter suppression efforts in many states, and the hateful rhetoric of many right-wing Republicans and their conservative Christian allies, the emergence of the next African American president may prove to be just as challenging, if not more so, than the election of President Obama.

I was a delegate for Barack Obama at the Democratic Convention in Denver in 2008. I stood with my son in the arena when Obama clinched the nomination. I was in the football stadium the next day when he gave his acceptance speech. I gathered with my congregation in the basement of our church in Cleveland, Ohio on election night, first when he carried Ohio and then when his election was announced. That was on November 4, 2008.

On November 4, 1930, one of my relatives, Edward Doneghy, went to register to vote for the first time at the age of 60. He was told on two occasions that "niggers do not and cannot vote in Kentucky," which is the state of origin for my family. When Doneghy said for a third time that he wanted to vote he was shot and killed by the registrar who pled self-defense against an unarmed man. That registrar shot and killed my great-great uncle because he wanted to prevent black people from gaining political power. Aldon Morris, writing in *Origins of the Civil Rights Movement,* made the point that keeping black people politically powerless was essential to the maintenance of the Jim Crow system of racial segregation. Doneghy was an existential threat to the stability of the status quo. It was exactly 78 years to the day when that registrar's worst fears came true—the election of an African American as this nation's president. While Barack Obama has performed splendidly as our president, nothing he does in office will match the sheer history-making fact of his election. From the slaves of George Washington to the slavery-ending struggle of Abraham Lincoln, the election of a descendant of Africa makes the election of President Barack Obama one of the epoch moments in all of American history.

Marvin A. McMickle, Ph.D., is president of Colgate Rochester Crozer Divinity School in Rochester, NY.

A ROLE MODEL FOR FAITH AND FAMILY

A United Methodist Perspective on Obama's Presidency

by Jim Winkler

When Barack Obama was elected the 44th president of the United States, I had been serving as general secretary of the United Methodist General Board of Church & Society for more than seven years. Right away, the transition team of the president-elect began inviting members of the faith community, including me and my staff, to participate in meetings on a wide variety of issues that would be facing the nation and the new president. At each meeting, the president-elect's representatives told us that Mr. Obama himself directed that the faith community have a "seat at the table." This set the tone for the next eight years, and it stood in direct contrast to the presidency of George W. Bush. Despite the fact both President Bush and Vice President Cheney were United Methodists and our denomination was the third largest religious body in the nation, there had been virtually no access for us to the White House.

Because of the controversy surrounding President Bush's Office of Faith-Based and Community Initiatives, many of us were surprised by and wary of President Obama's decision to retain it. Gradually, our concerns eased. The White House and executive agency faith-based staff did not play favorites. One conserva-tive Christian leader privately told me, for example, that he and others like him had been invited to the White House more times in the first year of Obama's presidency than they had been in all eight years of Bush's presidency.

Everyone in the faith community had access, although some clearly had more access and influence than others. The squeaky wheel certainly got the grease. Privileged access did not necessarily comport to the size and impact of religious bodies. Those of us who came from churches that did not toot their own horn but quietly went about everyday ministry to millions of the faithful; operated significant numbers of colleges, schools, seminaries, feeding programs, hospitals, and clinics; and who had deep, extensive, and longstanding connections around the globe were often overlooked by the Obama administration.

Although it should never be forgotten that President Obama is a politician—and many of his initiatives and policy choices were disappointing to the faith community—it gradually dawned on most of us that he was a man of deep faith who embraced many of our values and goals. In 2014, I became the president and general secretary of the National Council of Churches (NCC), a grouping of 38 member communions comprising more than 30 million Christians in over 100,000 local congregations. The NCC had long stood against racism, war, and poverty and had supported environmental justice and the rights of women. We deeply desired to see a nation that was more humane and just. President Obama himself had been formed in his Christian faith as a young community organizer in Chicago. He attended one of our congregations, Trinity United Church of Christ. The attacks on President Obama's personal faith were deeply disturbing to us, and we understood those assaults to be rooted in white racism.

Through his Christian faith and his faith in America, President Obama spoke eloquently to our nation for eight years in times of celebration and tragedy. I have no doubt he will be remembered as one of our greatest presidents. We will miss his leadership.

James Winkler is the President and General Secretary of the National Council of Churches.

A Merciful Heart and a Passion for Justice
by Sharon E. Watkins

It was at an off-the-record meeting in Chicago, early in the campaign, that I felt I saw your character—and your faith. The press had had a field day with the Rev. Jeremiah Wright's prophetic preaching and your church membership. At that Chicago meeting, the whole spectrum of Christian perspective was present. Conversation was wide-ranging and often tense. You never wavered in stating your belief. You never disrespected your questioner. You chose your words carefully for clarity. At the end we prayed.

Your presidency has had that same character: faithful, respectful, well-thought through. You have listened deeply and expected the best of those around you. You have wanted our nation and every person in it to prosper.

At the beginning of your historic administration, you made history again by asking a woman—me—to preach at the national prayer service, the first official act of your first day on the job. It signaled your commitment that the people's work should reflect the glorious diversity of the American people, including the majority who are female.

The scriptural focus of that service was Isaiah 58's "fast that God chooses," to "loose the bonds of injustice... to let the oppressed go free... to share bread with the hungry, and bring the homeless poor into a home." A merciful heart and a passion for justice are at the heart of our shared faith. The concern for the most vulnerable among us, however, is also the result of your deep-seated conviction, spoken so eloquently at your 2004 convention keynote, that we are one people, one nation, under God, indivisible.

This beautiful ideal is not always easy to embody. Many were surprised, given the enormity of the problems that faced us in early 2009 and the compelling margin of the electoral victory that your call to action met with resistance and even intransigence and personal insult. But your faith and your conviction that we are one nation called to a common mission of freedom and prosperity for all kept leading you back to the conversation table. You believed what you said in 2004: not red states and blue states, but the United States of America.

In spite of the headwinds, your administration and allies in Congress achieved much: health insurance for millions, strides in clean energy and reductions in emissions that pollute our air and superheat our planet, reversing the massive loss of jobs and increasing the net worth of millions of American families, stopping a massive oil spill and helping thousands of family businesses recover from the destruction, organizing a massive international response to Ebola, ending a failed 50-year policy of isolating Cuba—these are some of the achievements you shepherded to completion because of your faith in the oneness and fundamental goodness of the American people. These are moral issues. For you, they are deeply rooted in faith in God and in America.

In 2012, shortly after the murder of Trayvon Martin, you hosted an Easter breakfast. That time, you were the preacher! In this world, you said, there will be troubles, as our Lord knew. But we can keep our troubles in proper perspective as we remember Jesus. In his humanity, even Jesus struggled and doubted as he prayed at Gethsemane. By Christ's divinity, we realize that God's will is done; justice will come; love finally will prevail; life, not death, will have the final word.

This faith conviction has comforted you in the darkest hours. I think of Newtown, the enormous personal toll it took on you and on your staff, going to that school and meeting with the families of the precious children who were massacred. You turned to prayer. It wasn't publicly trumpeted for PR gain, but your staff reached out to faith leaders from the great diversity of American faith traditions and invited officials from across the administration to call in for a conference call prayer as we turned to God in our deep grief and mourning. I was reminded of that moment when you gave the eulogy for victims of racist hatred at Mother Emanuel. Those words, "Amazing Grace, how sweet the sound," rising from the depths of your grieving heart, were a powerful testament to our resurrection faith. The nation saw again your deep conviction that even in this most heinous act of evil, life triumphs over death, love has the final say.

Thank you, in your presidency, for embodying the abiding power of faith: faith in God and faith in the best of America.

Sharon E. Watkins is General Minister and President of the Christian Church (Disciples of Christ).

THE FAITH OF BARACK OBAMA

by Obery Hendricks, Ph.D.

I was among the first African-American religious leaders invited to join the faith advisory committee of the Obama presidential campaign. I accepted this invitation not for the prospect of joining a winning team, for, given our nation's tortured racial history. I did not imagine that a black man could be elected to the American presidency. The reason I joined the Obama campaign is because of the man I saw—a man who used his Harvard Law School degree not to get rich but rather to try to love his neighbors as himself by working to empower them as an organizer in some of Chicago's poorest neighborhoods. I noted the progressive political positions he had taken and the compassionate policies he proposed and supported as a state and national lawmaker. I listened to the content of his pronouncements and read the ethical vision underlying his words. I saw a devoted family man and a committed member of a Christian church that, with more than 80 community ministries (including senior citizen healthcare and housing, HIV/AIDS and hospice care, and 22 ministries for youth), is the very prototype of a Christian servant congregation.

These factors convinced me that Barack Obama was a man of deep faith who was fundamentally committed to building a more just, more equitable, more abundant, and more morally healthy nation for all Americans. That is why I chose to put my hand to the plow to work for the election of Barack Obama as President.

I have not always agreed with President Obama, but I've never doubted that his faith undergirded his decisions, even as he faced the disingenuous, rough-and-tumble world of politics and the fraught complexities of foreign diplomacy. Indeed, my respect for the President has grown as I've watched him struggle to provide healthcare for tens of millions of American children, women, and men at risk of bankruptcy, unrelieved suffering, even premature death because they lacked the healthcare that every civilized society should vouchsafe for its citizens. My respect for him has grown as I've watched his excruciating attempts at bipartisanship (the political equivalent of "love your enemies") and witnessed his refusal to gloat or cast aspersions after his hard-fought victories. My respect for President Obama has grown as I've watched his decency in the face of the lies and roiling hatred directed toward him and his family to a degree that has seldom been seen in the history of our republic. My respect for him soared when it became clear that—even as his political opponents spewed all manner of hateful invective against him, even demeaned his wife and young daughters in terms too indecent to be printed here—he refused to return evil for evil.

No person of good will can deny that in today's shamefully ugly political discourse, President Obama has acted in a much more Christian fashion than virtually all who have stooped to vilify him. For me, this is not only the measure of his faith. This is a measure of the man, the servant-leader, that his faith shaped him to be. Today, Barack Obama's greatness is seen only through a glass darkly. But I do believe that in the justice of God, the faithfulness of Barack Obama to the Gospel's call to love our neighbors as best we can will one day be seen in all its humility and in all its brilliance.

Obery M. Hendricks, Ph.D., is Professor of Biblical Interpretation at the New York Theological Seminary.

OBAMA, BIBLICAL TRUTH, AND POLITICAL RHETORIC
by Gay L. Byron, Ph.D.

For eight years, the people of the United States of America had a president with the "audacity to hope" and the courage to lead. Seeds for this audacity and courage were planted early in his life as he navigated different family networks, cultural realities, geographical contexts, and educational environments. These seeds were watered as he met different people along the way who provided opportunities for his innate leadership to come to the fore. Though many already knew of him through his influential community activism on the south side of Chicago and through his leadership as a state senator, it was his 2004 speech at the

Democratic National Convention that caught the attention of the American people and the political stakeholders throughout this country. "Who is this man?" I heard people ask. "Where did he come from?" they inquired with excitement. "He's the one who will be our next president," they affirmed without reservation. And so it was. By 2008, Barack Obama, after running a powerful campaign, broke through centuries of history, won the vote, and assumed the helm as president of the United States of America.

Presidents obviously must give up their privacy when they assume office—their freedom to use their cell phones or emails in ways in which they had been accustomed. They give up some of the places they used to visit or the friends they had met along the way. And often they give up the churches they used to attend. President Obama was forced to give up the pastor who nurtured him and led the spiritual base and home through which he gained knowledge and awareness of his history as a person of African descent and of his great potential to rise to the highest office of this country.

It was in March 2008 in the midst of the frenzy that had arisen about Mr. Obama's pastor, Rev. Jeremiah Wright, Jr., that I wrote an op-ed piece for a local newspaper in which, as a biblical scholar, I called attention to the unique hermeneutical (that is, interpretive) practices of preachers who represent what is known as the "Black Church Tradition." These preachers—such as Rev. William Barber, Bishop Vashti McKenzie, and Rev. Jeremiah Wright, Jr.—draw upon the Bible to provide commentary about the plight of African Americans and *all* Americans who are under the yoke of oppression. I emphasized at that time that those who are "untrained in the interpretive sophistication of African-American preachers and untutored in the historical relevance of the Black Church tradition" would be unable to comprehend the depth and breadth of the sermonic insights of these preachers.

In addition, the media does not help in its tendency to lift sound bites out of context and to mischaracterize the messages of influential black preachers as inflammatory or even racist.

It is ironic that President Obama appeals to biblical passages in several of his speeches, especially those that address matters pertaining to race, gun violence, and other tragedies that have plagued our country during his tenure. For example, his eulogy for the Charleston pastor Rev. Clementa Pinckney exemplified the president's command of the Bible, his deep sensitivity as a leader, and his great skill in connecting a particular moment with historical precursors and future possibilities. "The Bible," he said, "calls us to hope, to persevere, and have faith in things not seen." Indeed, this eulogy will be treasured as one of the powerful moments of his presidency. This was a message that he even closed by singing one of the great spiritual hymns of the church, "Amazing Grace."

Perhaps all of us might take a cue from this president who was nurtured in the rich biblical, prophetic, and spiritual tradition of the black church. Though sometimes he may not get the actual biblical citation correct (as in his misquoting the Gospel of John 3:18 for the epistle 1 John 3:18 in his speech about the police officers killed in Dallas), he will certainly be remembered as a president who has demonstrated how influential the Bible is in providing words of challenge, comfort, and hope in the midst of hatred, violence, and despair. I am grateful for President Barack Obama's audacity to hope and courage to lead. May his legacy of combining biblical truth with political rhetoric inspire the next generation of leaders in pulpits and even throughout the public square.

Gay L. Byron, Ph.D., is Associate Dean for Academic Affairs and Professor of New Testament at the Howard University School of Divinity in Washington, DC.

Mr. President

BRINGING FAITH COMMUNITIES TOGETHER
by Rev. Jennifer Butler

Only two weeks after taking office in 2009, President Barack Obama signed an executive order establishing the White House Office of Faith-based and Neighborhood Partnerships.

True to his campaign promises to unite Americans and bridge ideological divides and true to his experience as a faith community organizer, the president established a faith-based initiative that in appearance may have echoed his Republican predecessor but in practice carved out a more dynamic, diverse, innovative, and faithful approach to engaging religious and community groups.

As he appointed religious and community leaders to the first President's Advisory Council on Faith-Based and Neighborhood Partnerships, President Obama inspired us to collaborate, saying, "Instead of driving us apart, our varied beliefs can bring us together to feed the hungry and comfort the afflicted; to make peace where there is strife and rebuild what has broken; to lift up those who have fallen on hard times."

As a man of deep faith and experience, Obama knew that government could achieve so much more by binding faith leaders and community groups together. But this unconventional yet visionary approach to the faith-based program was not without controversy on the left and the right.

Conservative groups criticized the president's appointees. Progressive groups feared overreach by faith groups might compromise separation of church and state. Having often seen religious groups used politically, many progressives on principle opposed the very existence of a robust faith-based office. The office kept the same robust structure established by the George W. Bush administration with a central White House office and satellite offices in 12 government agencies working together to encourage partnerships between the government and religious and community groups for the delivery of social services.

Rather than focus on major liberal priorities, the goals of the program also included a mix of issues of interest to both conservative and progressive leaning faith communities: economic recovery, interfaith dialogue; encouraging responsible fatherhood and healthy families; and reducing unintended pregnancies, supporting maternal and child health, and reducing the need for abortion.

Most importantly, the first White House Council on Faith-based and Neighborhood Partnerships and all subsequent councils included ideologically, religiously, and racially diverse membership. The first Council of 25 members was composed of the broadest cross section of faith leaders. It included civil rights leader Rev. Otis Moss Jr.; Bishop Vashti McKenzie, the first woman elected as president of her historically black denomination's council of bishops; and prominent Muslims and Jews. But Joel Hunter, an evangelical, pro-life mega-church pastor from Florida, and Frank Page, past president of the Southern Baptist Convention, were among those who were unconventional appointments for a Democratic administration.

These councils over time helped build bridges among diverse leaders as well as put forth a number of common ground administrative actions that advance mutually shared policy concerns. The religious community had often been divided over many issues, particularly social concerns. Serving together in this capacity helped us all move to respect, deeper understanding, and unprecedented collaboration. While we may not agree on everything, our commonalities are so much greater than our differences and the Council focuses have accentuated those commonalities.

While the first Advisory Council focused on a wide range of topics, their report of recommendations observed this reality:

> *It is rare, if not unprecedented, for a governmental body to ask such a diverse group to seek common ground on a wide range of issues through sustained dialogue and deliberation. This process has been an education for Council members and, if we may say so, a blessing. Our report is the fruit of that labor. The understanding and relationships that have been built across lines of faith, belief, and political affiliation are equally important products of this work.*

The second Council focused on the issue of trafficking in persons as modern day slavery, which led to the increased attention and efforts, both within the government and in faith communities, to reduce human trafficking.

The third Council, which I chair, was called together to focus on poverty and inequality. Recommendations focused on increasing economic inequality; addressing race, justice and poverty; and strengthening government programs through more relational, holistic approaches. Ultimately, we have seen that government is working, and we have made recommendations for how the government, faith communities and community-based groups can do even more to address poverty and inequality in our communities.

President Obama has left a great legacy with regard to faith leadership, government partnerships, and moral leadership. Having helped our communities forge trusting relationships with each other and with government programs, we stand more ready than ever to lead this nation into a brighter future.

Rev. Jennifer Butler is CEO of Faith in Public Life and Chair of the President's Third White House Council on Faith-Based and Neighborhood Partnerships.

THE PROVIDENTIAL SHAPING OF OUR HISTORIC PRESIDENT

by Dr. Warren H. Stewart, Sr.

Proverbs 16:9 (NLT) offers, "We can make our plans, but the LORD determines our steps."

I do *not* believe Barack H. Obama would have become the first African-American president of the United States of America if the Lord had not prophetically prepared him by the influence of at least two African-American prophetic pastors, namely Dr. Lacey K. Curry, now Pastor Emeritus, Emmanuel Baptist Church; and Dr. Jeremiah A. Wright, Jr., now Pastor Emeritus, Trinity United Church of Christ; both from Chicago where the then-young community organizer met them.

President Obama was *not* brought up Christian as a child. His conversion to believing in Jesus Christ as his personal Savior happened to him as a young adult in the Windy City. If there was any religion to which he was exposed as a child, it was the Muslim faith of his Kenyan father and Obama's attending elementary school in Indonesia.

In Chicago, where this young, brilliant grassroots advocate spent significant time working with residents of inner-city neighborhoods, he was directed to meet the "spiritual chieftains" who were local pastors of Black churches. One of them was Pastor L. K. Curry of Emmanuel, who was one of the "elder" religious leaders. As Dr. Curry tells it, young Barack considered becoming a member of Emmanuel, but he told Obama that he would do better by going to meet Pastor Wright, one of his younger pastoral colleagues. At that time, Wright's leadership was a major prophetic voice among preachers in Chicago. Plus, Trinity's membership was exploding in growth; it had become the church Oprah Winfrey and other noted African-American leaders frequented.

Thus, Jeremiah A. Wright, Jr. became the most significant pastor-mentor of Obama, and God also used him to providentially shape America's first Black president. This one man of God influenced the future of the most powerful world leader by befriending him, discipling him into becoming a Christian, welcoming him as a member of Trinity, performing the wedding ceremony for Barack and Michelle, baptizing their two daughters, preaching his "unapologetically Christian and unashamedly Black" Sunday messages, and advising him of what it means to be Black in the USA. Mr. Obama so much as confirmed Wright's influence on him by writing an entire chapter about Trinity UCC and Pastor Wright in his first book, *Dreams from My Father.* In addition, his second book, *The Audacity of Hope*, was inspired by a message he had heard his pastor preach. Obama referred to that now famous title in his politically catapulting keynote address to the Democratic National Convention in 2004 as the first-term, junior U.S. Senator from Illinois.

The words of Joseph to his brothers, recorded in Genesis 50:20 (NLT) as his Egyptian leadership was drawing to a close, could be spoken by our *providentially shaped historic U.S. president*:

"As far as I am concerned . . . [God] brought me to this high position I have today so I could save the lives of many people."

Dr. Warren H. Stewart, Sr. is Senior Pastor of the First Institutional Baptist Church, Phoenix, AZ.

A GOOD FATHER

by Michael Wear

In the coming years, President Obama's legacy will be discussed and analyzed by historians, political strategists, policymakers, and everyday Americans. The impact of his policies in areas like health care, terrorism, nuclear weapons, climate change, and the economy will certainly draw much attention. These areas are important, of course, and deserve significant attention. However, in this space I want to consider the impact the president's example as a father and husband and his policy emphasis on fatherhood will have on our nation.

At a time of great cynicism regarding the institution of marriage, and rising questions about the value of fathers in particular, Barack Obama arrived on the national stage insisting on the singular value of the family. From the beginning—it was the central theme of his first book, *Dreams from my Father*—Obama affirmed the irreplaceable role of a father in a child's life. During his first campaign for the presidency, he spoke of the "hole in a young man's heart" that can be left by a father's absence and the policy implications of that absence. There is tremendous cultural power in a sitting president of the United States uttering the following words to fathers:

> *Let's be clear: Just because your own father wasn't there for you, that's not an excuse for you*

to be absent also—it's all the more reason for you to be present. There's no rule that says that you have to repeat your father's mistakes. Just the opposite—you have an obligation to break the cycle and to learn from those mistakes, and to rise up where your own fathers fell short and to do better than they did with your own children.

That's what I've tried to do in my life. When my daughters were born, I made a pledge to them, and to myself, that I would do everything I could to give them some things I didn't have. And I decided that if I could be one thing in life, it would be to be a good father.

Of course, the president's influence in the area of fatherhood was not only cultural. President Obama launched an initiative to promote responsible fatherhood that had concrete effects in this area. These efforts include reinvigorating the National Responsible Fatherhood Clearinghouse, providing tens of millions of additional dollars toward programs to promote fatherhood and healthy marriage, improving the child support system, and funding programs to help noncustodial and ex-offender fathers stay present in their child's life. The Obama administration released a report at the end of 2012 that detailed its efforts in this area, and it was a great honor of mine to work closely on these efforts during my time working in the White House. While we do not know much about what Barack Obama plans to do after he leaves the White House, he has already said he will continue to focus on these issues through My Brother's Keeper and the Obama Foundation.

We know that Barack Obama's race is part of what makes him exceptional in American history, and it will certainly play a role in how future generations consider his legacy. What is clear is that Barack and Michelle Obama's legacy will include their status not just as symbols and agents of the mainstreaming of black political power, but of a transcendent black love that renewed all of our imaginations for the sustaining, undeniable relevance of marriage and family in the twenty-first century. I believe we might look back on the Obama years and mark them as a time when our society's disenchantment with marriage was stemmed and a resurgence of fatherhood began. What a legacy to leave— to begin to fill the hole in America's heart in this new century.

Michael Wear led faith outreach for President Obama's re-election campaign and served in The White House Office of Faith-based and Neighborhood Partnerships during the president's first term. Michael is the author of the forthcoming book, *Reclaiming Hope: Lessons Learned in the Obama White House About the Future of Faith in America.*

No One Could Have Done It Better

by David A. Anderson

When President Barack Obama stood on the Capitol steps on that cold January morning of his inauguration, my wife and I stood among a sea of endless people caught up in the hope and change that Mr. Obama's victory to the highest office in the land afforded. For a young African-American pastor and his Asian wife, such a moment represented a monumental shift from a history of oppression and systemic bigotry in America toward a promise of hopeful equality and national unity.

To my surprise, the ugly head of opposition, veiled under the cloak of political conservatism, raised its head way too soon. The malicious attacks and verbal threats to unseat, not cooperate, and come against any and every proposed idea emanating from Mr. Obama set off a firestorm of disunity and ugliness that I couldn't have predicted.

As a daily radio talk show host during the afternoon drive on a conservative Christian station in the nation's capital, I was regularly fielding questions, comments, and even accusations about Mr. Obama being everything but a child of God. Yet I would again and again give testimony to the times I was in the room with the president, who would talk of his conversion, his Christian faith, and his respect for religious diversity. From National Prayer Breakfasts to Easter Breakfasts and high level meetings at the White House, Mr. Obama continued to reaffirm his faith again and again.

God couldn't have ordained as the first black president of the United States of America a more solid and sane man with the temperament, integrity, and discipline to handle such an enormous job as commander-in-chief than Barack H. Obama. I say this not because of his policy positions, some of which I vehemently disagreed with as an independent, non-partisan evangelical. My respect, however, comes because of his stature, character, steady hand of leadership, and accomplishments he achieved, even against vast opposition. In light of the defeat of Osama bin Laden, the Affordable Care Act, the removal of troops from Iraq and Afghanistan, the opening up of Cuba, and, most of all, the revitalization of an economy that was on life support and on its dying bed because of corporate greed spiraling America downward to the most crippling recession in modern history, the positive leadership and legacy of President Obama will be looked upon as historic for generations to come.

All of this without scandal and accomplished with class while honoring his beautiful wife and kids, who radiate dignity.

As Mr. Obama waves for the last time as president and peacefully transitions out of the most powerful office in the world, I can say that I am proud of the man that he is and the president that he was. The feelings of hope my wife and I had on that cold inaugural morning are still alive. But now we are more realistic and more sober about what it means to be a black leader in America. No one could have done it better than Mr. Barack Hussein Obama!

Dr. David Anderson is founder and president of the Bridge Leader Network (BLN) and Senior Pastor of Bridgeway Community Church in Columbia, MD.

THE NATION'S LAY PASTOR
by Dr. Harold A. Carter, Jr.

My initial reflection on two-term United States President Barack H. Obama is twofold: First, without a doubt, I assert that his term was God-breathed. Although President Obama had been a community organizer in Chicago, he certainly did not have the kind of extended political or governmental experience that would, on paper, afford him a green light to run for the most powerful political office in our nation, if not the world.

Of course, he began as a state senator and moved on to represent Illinois as a United States senator, but he had only served one term, just 300 days, before launching his presidential campaign. This man of color, born in Honolulu, Hawaii and graduate of Harvard Law School, where he was president of the *Harvard Law Review*, owes much to his keynote address given at the

2004 Democratic National Convention. This afforded him a national stage, and his persona, oration, and charisma catapulted him to another level of prominence.

Meanwhile, during the run up to the election, the Hillary Clinton for president machine was in motion and believed by most to be a done deal. Surprise. And the John McCain for president machine was in motion, capturing the votes of the Republican and conservative right. How dare this generally unknown young upstart with a mixed heritage (Kansas and Kenyan) and not enough dues paid have the audacity to "go for it" and call the nation to "Change We Can Believe In" and "Yes We Can"?

Then there was the race issue. Would this nation, steeped in its history of white male rule, ever accept and vote for a person of color? Plus the pro-Hillary media, along with the right-wing talk show personalities, along with the Republicans, discovered that he was a member of the Trinity U.C.C. Church, where Dr. Jeremiah Wright proudly professed the Gospel of Jesus Christ from his Africentric theological perspective. It seemed that too many forces were forming to hinder the grassroots "Obama for President" machine. But God….

Second, and more personal, is the fact that my late father, Dr. Harold A. Carter, "called it." My late mother, Weptanomah W. Carter, passed in 2006, but I recall my father saying to her, several years earlier, "there's something about that man," referring to then-Senator Obama. He said as much also to the New Shiloh Baptist Church congregation where he pastored for almost 48 years. Indeed, both of my parents could not have been more pro-Obama, as were many others who had not only been a part of the Civil Rights movement but also had a certain instinct and discernment that would only prove to be (and I return to my first reflection) providential.

Now, as for more of an analysis, I have come to appreciate the lay ministry leadership of President Obama. I use the term in the context of the church. There is a gentleman who's been a member at New Shiloh, where I presently serve, for over 35 years. He serves as an ordained deacon, but because of his ongoing devotion and faithfulness, participation, and service, my father often referred to him as a lay minister. Such is how I've seen our former president, especially leading up to his first election, his first year, and his final year. There was something ministerial about him: his words, his leadership, love of his family, and his convictions. I confess that I wish he would have owned this characteristic more, as I'm relatively sure that he knows he possesses it, or it, him.

Simply put, I believe God sent him (or set him up) to be our nation's pastor or lay pastor. At a time where we most needed shepherding—post two Bush administrations—he was hit hard by the recession, had to deal with the Iraqi war (and the associated tensions of that region), ongoing viable threats of terrorism (at home and abroad), and a Senate and House that conspired and implemented a "NO" policy against his administration. These things have ultimately proven to have been distractive. I do not contend that after eight years we are somehow worse off. I do, however, contend—even as he sought to personify his wife Michelle's words, spoken at the DNC's 2016 Convention, "When they go low, we go high"—that ultimately his best attributes (and I must add his swagger and his relationship with God) were allowed to be muted.

The effectiveness and genius of the Office of the President of the United States really isn't defined by the passing of laws, adherence to the Constitution, skillful negotiating, photo ops, or treatises. It's in being the voice of the nation's conscience. God knows we were lifted by such a voice early on. We heard it, periodically, trying to resonate. And as the campaign for the 2017 presidency came to a close, we heard it resonating again. I contend, however, that it was a voice that we needed throughout.

There was a distinct and markedly different tone in the president's campaign voice and his president-elect/presidential voice. I clearly recall saying to myself while listening to his 2008 acceptance speech, having been sworn in as our 44th president, that "something" must've happened. I'd grown accustomed to his stump speeches but also to his topical speeches, especially his speech on race, which he gave in Philadelphia in 2008 with such passion. Who could forget that he closed his speech with Hebrews 10:23: "Let us hold fast the profession of our faith without wavering; (for he is faithful that promised;)…"? I could only postulate that the consumption of the office had already begun to weigh upon him.

There were those who sought to brand President Obama in a negative, cynical way as a Messiah-type who asserted that his followers saw him as a kind of savior. This came from the conservative right and had no real merit. However, it seemed that the minority communities, especially African-Americans, were filled with hope and expectation for such a voice to have even greater impact on their behalf. Granted, it takes an awful lot of ego to want to be the president, but I've never thought that President Obama had a messianic complex. However, I will (with hesitancy) paraphrase St. John 10:4, that we (especially in the African-American and faith-based communities, minus the religious right) were willing to follow ("that") his voice, for we know "it" when we hear "it." And, yes, we were all the more willing to follow.

Dr. Harold A. Carter, Jr. is pastor of New Shiloh Baptist Church in Baltimore, Maryland.

THE ORDERED STEPS OF A GREAT MAN, PRESIDENT BARACK H. OBAMA!

by Unnia L. Pettus, Ph.D.

Psalm 37:23 states, "The steps of a good man are ordered by the Lord." There are two choices in life: having God order our steps in His will or ordering our own steps. Job 14:16 tells us God numbers our steps, and 31:4 that He counts all our steps, and in 34:21 that He sees all our goings. When God orders, anything other than what He orders becomes out of order. Spurgeon said, "When this pilot undertakes to steer their course, their vessel shall never split upon the rock, run upon the sands, or spring a leak, so as to sink in the seas. To be sure, He will see them safe in their harbor."

In interviews throughout his political career, President Barack H. Obama has affirmed his belief in Jesus. As the world's most powerful leader, he has spoken openly of his Christian faith and a personal relationship with Jesus Christ. He has also claimed he has "absolutely" read the Bible and has "an ongoing conversation with God." In an interview with *Cathedral Age* in August 2012, President Obama discussed the growth of his faith since taking office. He said, "My faith is a great source of comfort to me. I've said before that my faith has grown as president. This office tends to make a person pray more; and as President Lincoln once said, 'I have been driven to my knees many times by the overwhelming conviction that I had no place else to go.'"

Not everyone can say a U.S. president helped save their lives, **but I can**. In January 2012, I had a major stroke with right-side paralysis due to a blood clot. I was devastated beyond words because I could no longer write or walk, nor take care of myself in any manner. My thoughts were unclear and my memory damaged; I had to focus on a new way of living. I was told that I shouldn't expect to ever be back to normal or at least not to expect a full recovery for years to come. I heard the physician's diagnosis, but I knew ultimately my fate was in God's hands, so I prayed and kept my faith. I begged God to allow me to be able to recover enough to work to get President Barack Obama reelected in November 2012, and He granted my request months earlier.

After nearly a year of painful physical and vocational therapy, I could use a wheelchair and roll into the Obama For America DC headquarters to be a part of history once again. From that wheelchair, and, later, using a walker, I served as the Core Team Fellow for African American Faith Outreach for the Obama for America (OFA) DC Campaign. This was nothing but a miracle from God and an answered prayer.

After his election, I enthusiastically supported the passage of health care reform. After five presidents over a century failed to create universal health insurance, President Obama signed the Affordable Care Act (2010). I know how important it is as a disabled African American clergy leader who still faces health care and financial challenges. It's been a Godsend to more than 32 million uninsured Americans beginning in 2014 and mandates a suite of experimental measures to cut health care cost growth, the number one cause of America's long-term fiscal problems. To me, this has been the greatest accomplishment of his administration and legacy to date. President Obama is an angel to me!

Reverend Unnia L. Pettus, Ph.D., is Founder and CEO, Nobody But God Ministries.

A TRUE FIRST FAMILY
by Dr. D. Darrell Griffin

As I reflect on the presidency of Barack Obama, I quickly recall moments in which his decisions, policies, and character have touched my soul. Beyond his appropriate, relevant, and timely actions for our country and the irreversible global village, which includes all countries on the globe, an overarching contribution of his presidency upon my life remains his genuine "family values."

President and Mrs. Obama and their daughters have been a true "First Family." All American citizens can be very proud of their formidable example of love, care, support, poise, and dignity. The Obama daughters, Sasha and Malia, always conducted themselves with grace, composure, refined manners, and generosity. Naturally, they glean these invaluable attributes from their beloved mother, who as First Lady of the United States, personified beauty, formal education, loyalty, and dedication that husbands desire in wives and children need in their mothers. President Obama persistently speaks favorably of his mother-in-law, thereby revealing an authentically close relationship.

These positive and real images of the Obamas elevate the perception of African American families within popular discourse and culture. Moreover, they silence uninformed and insincere critics who offer platitudes and vapid rhetoric regarding family values when their lives reflect a completely opposite way of living. This powerful legacy of love, admiration, affirmation, and service within your primary relationships that the Obama family exemplifies will inspire, encourage, and empower many future generations of diverse Americans who greatly desire a similar family setting.

Currently, I serve as the senior pastor of a congregation within the Evangelical Covenant Church of America, a moderately conservative denomination with Swedish origins. I also have the privilege and distinction of having served as Chairman of the Executive Board of our denomination; not surprisingly, I am the first African American to be elected to the position. Most regrettably, on several occasions I overheard ministerial and administrative colleagues inappropriately characterize President Obama as "the anti-Christ" because of his polices relating to marriage equality, healthcare, and size and role of government. Despite their virulent disagreement with his policies and vision for the country and world, this group of church leaders is unable to attack President Obama regarding his personal example of "family values." In the last four decades of American politics, the Republican Party and the "Religious Right," inclusive of various evangelical denominational leaders, maintained a monopoly in defining and validating "family values." However, President Obama, hailing from an ideologically opposite spectrum, shattered this misconception and misguided practice with the integrity of personal marital and parental example and consistency and generosity of his policies, which respect all people as children of God. As the president smashes this golden calf of public discourse, political, social, and religious conservatives scramble aimlessly to find another idol.

Interestingly, I began to understand more fully the amazing impact of President Obama's positive family image when my son, Myles, who was then eight or nine years old, happened to point it out to me. As we watched a portion of a speech that President Obama was delivering, my son remarked, "Look, Daddy, it's the President of the United States! He is just like you." Both puzzled and shocked, I responded, "What do you mean by the President is just like me?" With a child's innocence, my son said, "He wears a suit just like you. He gives speeches just like you. He is a daddy like you and he has the same skin color as you. But thank you for being my 'Daddy President' like President Obama." "Daddy President," I said aloud. My son fired back in an affirming voice, "You are the president of our family!" Fascinatingly, Miles's observations revealed a side of the president's service and legacy that I previously overlooked. I had not realized the positive role model as a husband and father that President Obama had on Myles and on countless millions of children and their families.

Similar to most African American children, my sons daily combat the media exaggerations and popular culture portrayals of them as violent criminals lurking to prey upon hapless and unsuspecting victims. These distortions fail to report how far removed many of these children and youth are from any criminally violent connections or social dilemmas. These wholesale pathological depictions are usually silent about the pivotal role of fathers, caretakers, providers, mentors, and community leaders who commit their lives to saving their children and improving their quality of life. These erroneous illustrations of African American males perpetuate harmful stereotypes that undermine any efforts for social, political, and economic progress within the Black community and throughout American society. More harmfully, this persistently negative coverage poisons the minds and hearts of young people, possibly furthering rank bias and prejudice and preventing them from establishing more progressive and mutually beneficial relationships across racial, ethnic, cultural, religious, linguistic, educational, and class lines.

More dishearteningly, these media and popular culture images desecrate the respect and role of African American males in the eyes of their own sons and daughters, in addition to society. Most disappointingly, many Black men internalize these pathological characterizations, thereby defeating ambitions, discarding dreams, and destroying character and hope. These demeaning and derogatory societal assumptions about Black males seek to demolish their personhood and to undermine any consideration of their potential to make contributions to humankind. As a husband, father, leader of the United States of America and free world, and inspirational figure within developing countries, President Barack Obama contradicted these diabolical images. Any perpetuation of them rightly deserves immediate and unequivocal condemnation of all people of good faith.

As an African-American father, I adamantly deplore the foregoing and enduring portrayals of Black males as irresponsible, lazy, inherently violent and criminal, and highly sexual. In President Obama, my sons see a Black male father and husband, not only in their house but in the White House, who is the exact opposite of those stereotypes. His formidable and unquestioned example offers audacious hope to future generations of young Black boys as they become men. Should they fail to achieve their potential, apply themselves, and actualize their natural endowments due to these lingering and ignorant assaults on their characters, American society suffers. Our economy loses their productivity. The absence of their contributions significantly diminishes research, academics, innovation, and fine and performing arts in addition to athletics and entertainment. These misconceptions create internal and existential breeding grounds of hopelessness, despair, and mistrust.

Reversing and nullifying harmful classifications of African American males is essential to improving Black marriages and families. Daily, throughout this country—from the Eastern coastal inner cities to the heartland and plain states to the pockets of African Americana in the Pacific Northwest down to border towns of the Gulf Coast—nameless and countless

Black males anonymously emulate President Obama's example. Wholeheartedly, I pray the legacy of his incredible presidency will continually and permanently change the heretofore negative trajectory of young African American males and the image of the African American family.

Before his inauguration, President Obama published an open letter to his daughters in *Parade*, a weekly magazine insert within most Sunday papers throughout the country, describing his fatherly desires for them and every child in America: "to grow up in a world with no limits on your dreams and no achievements beyond your reach." I share his hope for my sons and all children in the global village. The presidency of Barack Obama gives us a new image to embrace: formally educated, successful, and faithful African American men in marriage and family. Accordingly, his magnanimous example truly yields an audacity to hope that his heartfelt wishes for his daughters are within our reach as well.

Dr. D. Darrell Griffin is Senior Pastor at Oakdale Covenant Church in Chicago, IL.

SOMETIMES SEEING IS BELIEVING
by The Reverend Jonathan C. Augustine, J.D., M.Div.

"Now faith is the substance of things hoped for, the evidence of things not seen." —*Hebrews* 11:1 (KJV)

"[B]ecause thou hast seen me, thou hast believed: blessed are they that have not seen, and yet they have believed." —*John* 20:29 (KJV)

I grew up in a Black family during the 1970s and 80s in inner-city New Orleans. Like so many Black children brought up in the Deep South at that time, I was repeatedly taught about the importance of faith. Indeed, the popular passage from Hebrews that "faith is the substance of things hoped for, the evidence of things not seen" was drilled into my mind and subconscious.

To be perfectly candid, because of what can only be termed as dysfunction in my childhood home, and because of the types of homes in which my first cousins grew up, I did not have a personal familiarity with the "traditional" Black family. Please understand that my intended use of the term "traditional" contains absolutely no misogynistic or sexist undertones. My own mother worked as an educator and sacrificed to provide for me and my sister, notwithstanding the fact I grew up in a two-parent home. Instead, my use of the term "traditional" is intended to describe a Black family where the husband and wife work collaboratively at raising children while simultaneously pursuing common goals that are in the best interests of the family.

Regrettably, based on my intended use of the term, my adolescent exposure to a traditional Black family was limited to the Huxtables, a two-parent family with whom I shared many special moments, courtesy of NBC, over the course of eight years. Now, as an adult living in a blended family—arguably the new definition of traditional—my wife, Michelle, and I have faith that what they see not only in us but also in the Obama family will influence their personal notions of what a traditional Black family is supposed to be.

In playing on Hebrews' popular passage about faith, as I reflect on the Black America I knew as a child, I could only have faith that traditional Black families actually existed, considering they were not something I had personally seen. In reflecting on today, however, notwithstanding my children's personal familiarity with my definition of "traditional," I am delighted by the blessing of what they have seen for the last eight years—the vast majority of their young lives—in how special a traditional Black family can be. This overwhelmingly positive influence, in the form of a faith that has come to fruition, has redefined expectations not only for me but for an entire generation. This has been possible only because of President Barack Obama and the overwhelmingly positive influence resulting from his "traditional" First Family.

In John 20, as Jesus appears to his disciples sometime after the resurrection, Thomas becomes overwhelmed with amazement, and *only* after seeing Jesus professes his belief. In many regards, I am much like Doubting Thomas. Because I have now seen the positive influences of a traditional Black Family—where both mother and father are attentive to their children and collaboratively work to better their children's lives—I now believe. Because I have also seen mutual support, encouragement, and a familial pursuit of excellence, I now believe. Because I have seen a Black man who is secure enough in his masculinity to be openly affectionate with his family, while simultaneously being tough enough to take out international terrorists who threatened his family's safety, I now believe. Indeed, I am quite a bit like Doubting Thomas because I had never before seen a Black family so loving, but at the same time so driven for personal and professional excellence, that I can now believe traditional is in fact possible. In many regards, therefore, I am proud to be like Doubting Thomas. Because I have now seen, I also have new standards on what should be normal and "traditional" in Black America. More importantly, my children can also believe because of everything they have seen.

I give special thanks to the Obamas for not only bringing my childhood faith to fruition, but more importantly for showing my children and an entire generation what a "traditional" Black family should be.

God bless the Obama family, and God bless the United States of America.

Rev. Jonathan C. Augustine is the senior pastor of Historic St. James African Methodist Episcopal Church in New Orleans, LA. and the National Chaplain of Alpha Phi Alpha Fraternity, Inc.

WHAT MATTERS THE MOST
by Carlton Reed

As I reflect on the presidency of President Barack Obama and what it has meant to me, there are a number of things I could mention. I could mention the accomplishment of being the first African-American in history to be elected president of the United States. I could mention that for the first time in our nation's history, every African-American boy or girl, upon their birth, has the opportunity to ascend to the highest office in the land. I could mention the achievement of winning the Nobel Prize, thus being one in the company of a long line of history shapers. Although all of these are great accomplishments, these are not the ones I will focus on. The one that perhaps makes the greatest impact is not one that many might choose, but is that of being a president who is a devoted husband and father.

What impact do the actions of a president make upon his family watching him? As the leader of the free world, there are a number of very important activities that could occupy his day, but the impact of being present as a devoted husband and loving father to his daughters will be remembered long after his presidency. I would like to suggest that being a good father and husband may be one of the godliest things a man can do. To see the president being present as a loyal and devoted husband with the First Lady and his daughters, Sasha and Malia, speaks volumes. When all of the smoke clears, the presidential term ends, and all of the fanfare has waned, I imagine that the intentional time taken to be there for his family will have mattered most. I thank you for your service to our country, for being intentionally present for your family, and for loving your wife and children. God bless you as you transition to this next phase of your life.

I'd like to leave you with a poem written by another president, Theodore Roosevelt. It was great then, and it's still great. It reads:

> *It is not the critic who counts; not the man who points out how the strong man stumbles, or where the doer of deeds could have done them better. The credit belongs to the man who is actually in the arena, whose face is marred by dust and sweat and blood; who strives valiantly; who errs, who comes short again and again, because there is no effort without error and shortcoming; but who does actually strive to do the deeds; who knows great enthusiasms, the great devotions; who spends himself in a worthy cause; who at the best knows in the end the triumph of high achievement, and who at the worst, if he fails, at least fails while daring greatly, so that his place shall never be with those cold and timid souls who neither know victory nor defeat.*

God bless you, President Obama.

Carlton Reed is a speaker, author, and founder of Carlton Reed Ministries.

An Inspiration to Children

by Fr. Kenneth Taylor

As the administration of President Barack Obama comes to an end, it is good to have this opportunity to look back on his presidency from a faith perspective. President Obama came into the White House as a strong family man. Devoted to his wife and children and knowing what life would be like in the White House, he even had the children's grandmother live with them to make sure that everyone could stay grounded. We see so much going on in all areas of society around us that destroy family life, so it has been refreshing to see the First Family able to maintain their integrity throughout these eight years. Faith tells us that the family is still the building block of society.

When President Obama came into office, he stated that he wanted to bring diplomacy back to the forefront of our foreign policy. At that time we were in a state of war, and as he leaves office we continue to be in a state of war. So it may seem as though this hope was not fulfilled. But with a closer look, we can see that great strides were made in using diplomacy instead of fear, threats or force, as part of our foreign policy. During his time in office, nations have come together several times and worked out agreements, treaties, and understandings on a number of controversial and even contentious issues. History will tell how successful these efforts will be. But it does show that when the effort is made it is possible to work with others, even those we may not agree with.

What do you do when there are those who set out to oppose everything you are trying to do? That is the question President Obama has had to live with throughout his term. Those who opposed him in Congress decided they would block everything he would try to do. This can be seen in the record number of filibusters and the record number of nominees who were not confirmed during his administration. But we never saw President Obama strike back in revenge or in spite. He kept working on his agenda; when one way was blocked he would find another way to get things done. The Gospels tell us that if we strive to live out our faith, there will be obstacles in our way. Our response should be to stay strong, remain faithful, and keep moving forward. We see all that in President Obama. I am the pastor of a Catholic Church in Indianapolis that has a school that is predominantly African-American. A most important part of President Obama's legacy is the effect it has had in the lives of our schoolchildren. His being president has been nothing but an inspiration to them. Here is an African-American man who has achieved success and, even facing the challenges he did, was still able to live by the values that we work so hard to teach.

Fr. Kenneth Taylor is pastor at Holy Angels Catholic Church and St. Rita Catholic Church in Indianapolis, IN and President of the National Black Catholic Clergy Caucus.

CARRYING FAITH INTO THE WHITE HOUSE
by Wesley Granberg-Michaelson

Every president must navigate the relationship of religious faith, both public and private, to the presidency. Barack Obama did this with exceptional grace, wisdom, and skill, which will set a precedent for those who follow. While other accomplishments in his policies as well as changes in the national consciousness will be widely noted in his legacy, his model of appropriating religious faith in the practice of his presidency, while often overlooked, will become historically a distinguishing feature of his eight years in office.

Abraham Lincoln once said, "My concern is not whether God is on our side; my greatest concern is to be on God's side." But many U. S. presidents almost instinctively have tried to use religion to bless and bolster their political power. The danger is that faith and its prophetic message gets reduced to "civil religion," capable of little more than baptizing the authority of the established order.

President Obama resisted that temptation. And he gave clear signals of his approach to the intersection of faith and politics in an historic and revealing speech in 2006 to a conference of Call to Renewal in Washington, D.C., sponsored by Sojourners. "Secularists are wrong," Senator Barack Obama said, "when they ask believers to leave their religion at the door before entering into the public square. Frederick Douglas, Abraham Lincoln, William Jennings Bryant, Dorothy Day, Martin Luther King—indeed the majority of great reformers in American history were not only motivated by faith, but repeatedly used religious language to argue for their cause."

So President Obama carried his faith into the White House, knowing its potential to catalyze reform. But he also recognized, as he said in 2006, how "democracy demands that (those) religiously motivated translate their concerns into universal, rather than religion-specific, values." So the use of his Christian faith, with its language, metaphors, and even songs, was never employed in sectarian ways. Rather, it framed a broader story, one that included those of other faiths and even no faith.

We saw this again and again, beginning perhaps in the Philadelphia speech on race during the 2008 campaign, and then in Cairo, speaking to the world's Muslim community. In Oslo, reflecting on the ethical dilemmas of power and the pursuit of peace, and in Charlotte, where undoubtedly he was the first president to sing "Amazing Grace" as part of a speech. In so many settings, President Obama became "Pastor-in-Chief" in ways reminiscent of Lincoln, understanding the social weight of grief and human suffering. Undoubtedly, his experience in the black church provided the portal for exercising this gift to the nation.

But make no mistake. President Obama's legacy of faith and politics was not merely rhetorical. It also involved practice. Most notable was the support he gave to the Office of Faith-based and Neighborhood Partnerships. That initiative was begun by President George W. Bush, often to the dismay of some secular Democrats. But President Obama had the wisdom to broaden and deepen this effort. After eight years, with the leadership of Joshua Dubois and then Melissa Rogers, dialogue and partnerships with religious groups have been imbedded in many cabinet-level departments. Still respecting boundaries between church and state, the government's cooperation with faith-based initiatives is now recognized as an intrinsic component in implementing national policies. That's part of Barack Obama's legacy.

Barack Obama also developed meaningful ways for a president to relate to and celebrate directly with America's diverse religious communities. He began celebrating annually a Jewish Passover Seder in the White House. He celebrated Ramadan with Muslims holding Iftar dinners (as had Presidents Bush and Clinton). With Hindus, he was the first U. S. President to celebrate Deepavali, the festival of lights, in 2009. And in 2016, for the first time a president acknowledged the Buddhist holiday of Vesak.

But perhaps of special personal meaning, he began a yearly tradition of hosting an Easter Prayer Breakfast in the White House for Christian leaders. Unlike the annual National Prayer Breakfast for several thousand held at the Washington Hilton, this event gathered a couple of hundred from the diversity of Christianity for food and fellowship around tables, music, a speaker, and then words from President Obama, which always were like a window into his heart.

In one meeting between denominational leaders and President Obama in the Roosevelt Room of the White House, we shared about poverty, Cuba, and the Middle East. An aide came to say it was time for him to leave. But he turned to us and said, "Aren't we going to pray?"

No President can ever withstand the Bible's prophetic message holding power accountable to justice. God's demands require more than any President can obey. Yet Barack Obama brought his faith with him into the White House, allowing it to be expressed, and even to blossom, in ways marked by authenticity and spiritual power. His desire was to seek even partial and imperfect ways in which he could ask not whether God was on our side, but whether we could be judged as leaning toward God's side.

Wesley Granberg-Michaelson served as General Secretary of the Reformed Church in America for 17 years, from 1994-2011. He played a leading role in establishing Christian Churches Together in the USA and is known globally for his ecumenical leadership.

Mr. President

A Vision and Legacy of Faith and Trust
by Joshua DuBois

Two years after graduating from college, a young man named Barack Obama was hired by the Developing Communities Project, a church-based organization on the South Side of Chicago funded by the Catholic Campaign for Human Development. The organization served families who had lost jobs, income, and often hope as well after steel plants closed down and workers were laid off. As the new executive director, Obama set about partnering with religious leaders in Chicago to organize job training programs, provide college tutoring to young people, and advocate for tenants' rights.

In this work, the future president saw a vision for how faith and civic organizations could form partnerships with government to meet real human needs, serve the common good, and restore dignity for all.

After the 2008 Presidential election, that vision and those experiences—and many others along the way—formed the ethos and mission of President Obama's newly reconstituted federal faith-based and community initiative, the White House Office of Faith-based and Neighborhood Partnerships.

I served as President Obama's first executive director of this office. He and I examined previous efforts at faith-based and nonprofit partnerships in both the Bill Clinton and George W. Bush administrations. We looked at what worked well and what could be improved. And we charted a course that would seek to bring together communities of faith and government in an interwoven tapestry focused on meeting human needs.

As President Obama's time in office comes to a close, it is worth noting how his faith-based initiative has produced results for the nation and the world, especially for our brothers and sisters in need. A few highlights:

1) Robust development of public-private partnerships that go beyond dollars and cents

Coming into office, President Obama noticed a tension between faith communities and the federal government because of an expectation that the only basis for relationship between the two was federal funding—dollars and cents. The president invited faith organizations to become partners, rather than just grantees, of the federal government. While federal funding remained, we also expanded our work into many successful "civic partnerships" that were not financially based. We helped religious and government groups work together on common goals, including job training, feeding hungry kids in the summer time, supporting juveniles who have been incarcerated, mobilizing interfaith service teams on college campuses, combating human trafficking, turning around failing public schools, stepping in to help when a disaster hits a community, expanding religious and cultural awareness in foreign diplomacy, and helping community members access affordable healthcare. These civic partnerships will be a lasting legacy of President Obama's administration.

2) A legal framework that will guide engagement between faith communities and government for years to come

In President Obama's first term, we constituted a new advisory council for Faith-based and Neighborhood Partnerships—non-government leaders in the faith-based and nonprofit spaces that proposed legal frameworks for the work of the faith-based office. Then, in the president's second term under the leadership of Melissa Rogers, the White House Office of Faith-based and Neighborhood Partnerships implemented many of these legal and constitutional principles and criteria for the partnerships formed between faith-based groups and government agencies. By working with each federal agency to ensure these principles were implemented and practiced, Americans of all faiths or none could be assured that their freedoms were respected and protected in this administration and in administrations to come.

3) Increased communication and collaboration between faith and government leaders in the policymaking process

On a range of issues, including immigration, budget negotiations, criminal justice reform, veterans' assistance, foreign policy, and more, faith communities were engaged in the policymaking process. Their diverse thoughts and opinions were taken closely into account, creating unprecedented alignment between the federal government and neighborhood and faith-based groups who know communities most.

Beyond the policy specifics, though, I have had the honor of knowing President Obama's heart on his own faith and the role of religion in the public square. I saw him at the annual Easter Prayer Breakfast give passionate, personal speeches about how his Christian faith informed his life. I saw him welcome leaders from diverse traditions—from the annual White House Passover Seder to the Iftar gathering to the first ever White House event for Diwali—in warm embrace. I watched as he gathered with a table of faith leaders in the Roosevelt Room of the White House and stretched his hand to grasp Dr. Barbara Williams-Skinner's hand in prayer. I journeyed with him up the side of a mountain to meet with Rev. Billy Graham at the great leader's home—the first sitting president to do so. Melissa and I prayed with him each year on his birthday with a small group of other leaders.

And every morning, I had (and continue to have) the honor of sending a brief devotional message to the president to begin his day in reflection and prayer. Our president may not always wear his faith on his sleeve, but he has walked the Christian walk over the last eight years, in ways public and private, and has extended his arms to people of all faiths—and no faith at all—to join with him in the project of American renewal.

Joshua DuBois is the former Special Assistant to President Obama and Executive Director of the White House Office of Faith-based and Neighborhood Partnerships.

"BEHIND-THE-SCENES" REFLECTIONS

MEMORIES OF A COMPASSIONATE LEADER

by Joel Hunter

As a citizen, my standard for our president is this: is he or she competent to hold the office? The presidency of the United States demands an intellectual prowess, a strategic capability, and a competence in multitasking on a level not comparable to any other calling. As a pastor, though, my hope is that our president would be one who would "look out for the interests of others," who "empties Himself, taking on the form of a servant." My joy is to support someone who prioritizes all people, especially those not normally included.

My personal memories of President Obama will always be of his great compassion and his unshakable desire to help the most vulnerable among us. The terms "civil rights" and "human rights" are legal terms; his thinking was always characterized by personal compassion.

In my first phone conversation with him, shortly after he declared his candidacy for the office of the presidency, we talked about the untapped resources of people in the faith communities across our country: they could be the personal support to poor and struggling people, which could augment government aid.

My first prayer with him came before a presidential debate. After asking Senator Clinton a question and listening to her very good answer, I was asked if I would go pray with Senator Obama. Expecting to be in a large crowd of pastors, I was surprised to find it was just him and me in a hallway. He had been beaten up by the press that week, but when I spoke of him having a rough week, his response was something to the effect, "Not really. The people out of work, the single moms, the sick...now *they've* had a rough week."

My first prayer time with him in the Oval Office was after a personal conversation with him about faith and family. I asked him how I could pray for him. His response was, "Let's pray for our country. There are a lot of people hurting out there."

When my five-year-old granddaughter was diagnosed with a brain tumor (that would take her life ten weeks later), one of the first calls I got started like this, "Joel, this is Barack. I just found out about your granddaughter. What can I do to help?" When I said there was no medical treatment effective for this type of tumor, my voice began to break. He then began to be *my* pastor by reminding me to depend on the God who does not abandon us.

In 2012 I was driving with my wife, Becky, and got a call on my cell. The president told me about an interview he just had done with ABC in which he gave his support to gay marriage. He knew me to be a conservative pastor so he was not surprised when I said, "Mr. President, I don't see that in the Bible." His response was something like, "I know, but we are talking about *civil* marriage, a civil right for everyone, not about a specifically religious interpretation." He then told me about a young gay man who worked in the West Wing, whom he passed every day, and for whom he wondered, "Why can't he have a marriage, too?" It revealed to me once more that President Obama always thinks with compassion and equality when it comes to those who have not been included. Even the reason for the call was compassionate. His thought: "I wanted to tell you immediately because I know you take a lot of hits for our relationship, and I knew you would probably get beat up over this." So he was being protective of me, whether or not I agreed with his decision.

My memories of President Obama's term in office will be not merely of how good he was on so many issues: peace, protecting the environment, expanding health care to so many millions, overseeing the economy's recovery from near-Depression level dysfunction to stability and health, addressing the racism in our systems and in our hearts, and so many other legacy initiatives. My memories will be of something even more profound and lasting: he was a president who loved well. He loved his family well (every time I asked about Michelle and the girls his eyes lit up). He loved his team well, forever crediting those around him. He loved his enemies well, seldom disrespecting them even in private conversations. But he especially loved those not already included, in great part because he believes in a God who included him by grace. He is still always choosing to extend that grace to others.

Joel Hunter is the senior pastor of Northland, A Church Distributed.

WORKING TIRELESSLY FOR CHANGE

by Cynthia L. Hale

I was first introduced to President Barack Obama from afar as he dazzled the nation at the 2004 Democratic Convention. In that speech, he reminded us of our unity as Americans and of the fact that, despite all the discord and struggle that are a part of our collective history, there has always been a dogged optimism in the future that he referred to as "the audacity of hope."

It was two years later, when I read his book *The Audacity of Hope*, that I had my first real glimpse into the soul of our president. What arrested me was his sharing of the path to the Senate from the state of Illinois. He spent time traveling the state "listening" to people of all races, religions, and classes. He found a common thread in their hopes and dreams—dreams for jobs that pay a living wage, affordable healthcare, a quality education for their children, and the opportunity for those same children to go to college. He listened to the people as they shared their desire for safe communities and the ability to retire with dignity and respect.

In 2007, I received a call from a young man, Paul Monteiro, who asked if I would serve as co-chair of Women in Ministry for Obama with Bishop Vashti McKenzie. Obama was campaigning to become the 44th president of the United States of America. I asked Paul if I could have a few days to pray about the assignment. He said "yes" and suggested that I also participate in a call with the Senator's wife, Michelle Obama. Hearing Mrs. Obama speak helped me make up my mind. What I realized on that call was that not only was President Obama prepared and committed to working tirelessly for change in our nation, but his wife was as well. In electing Barack Obama, we would be getting a savvy African-American man with swagger and a beautiful, equally intelligent, African-American woman, Michelle Obama.

What has given me great respect for and confidence in the leadership of our president is that throughout his tenure, he hasn't just listened to the stories and concerns of the people. He was intimately involved in doing whatever it took to do something about them. This was made undeniably clear to me as I sat in the Roosevelt room on one of numerous occasions with groups that he personally entertained there. During one of those times, while the rest of the city of Washington was shut down because of a snowstorm and the president could have taken a day off, he met with and addressed the questions of the members of the Commission on White House Fellowships. We discussed everything from affordable health care to My Brother's Keeper, a program for Black and Brown men and boys. I suggested that he might use a White House fellow to help manage and oversee the program. He smiled and said he would think about it. Later I learned that he assigned two of our Fellows to work extensively with the My Brother's Keeper program.

While there are those who would accuse his administration of trying to take over and do it all, what I have appreciated is that our president has given the people of this great nation "hope" in the fact that government cares about its people. He has also given us the help we all need to live our lives with dignity and respect.

While we realize that he was elected to serve all Americans, the president has supported the African-American community in amazing ways. His initiatives include: helping African-American students get a quality education from cradle to career, strengthening Head Start, spurring 46 states to raise K-12 standards through the Race to the Top Initiative, making college more affordable by doubling Pell Grant Scholarships to support African-American students, and securing millions in additional funding to historically Black colleges and universities. President Obama pushed for and signed the Affordable Care Act, which has provided millions of African-Americans with health coverage and will provide all Americans health care when it is fully implemented.

I have great respect for President Barack Obama and the way that he has conducted himself while in office amidst great disrespect and a lack of cooperation from those elected to help govern our nation. He governed with integrity. I know that is because our president is a man of great faith, honesty, and genuine spirituality.

Cynthia L. Hale is Senior Pastor at Ray of Hope Christian Church in Decatur, GA.

AN ORDINARY KIND OF GUY

by Bishop Vashti McKenzie

I had met Barack Obama from afar, every year coming to the Congressional Black Caucus Annual Legislative Conference. From afar, I heard of him as friends, neighbors, and other AMEs in Illinois began to talk about this state senator who was going to run for the United States Senate and expressed their excitement. I thought, "Why are you excited?" He was not mentioned along with the other persons who are usually discussed when you talk about social justice issues. Whenever you talk about social justice, human rights, and civil liberties, there are about four or five people that are always mentioned: Jesse Jackson, Al Sharpton, and any members of the King family. Yet my friends were talking about State Senator Barack Obama.

At the Congressional Black Caucus dinner, everyone would say, "There he is. There's Senator Obama." And I was like, "Who? Where?" He would just walk in and say "hi" to everyone, smile, shake hands, then sit down at the table. There was no entourage. There was no security. He was just like one of the crowd, an ordinary guy. You would nod and say, "Hello, Senator, how are you?" He didn't know you from Adam and would just sit down.

Then one Sunday I was preaching The Seven Last Words on Easter Sunday at Trinity United Church of Christ in Chicago. Dr. Jeremiah Wright, Jr. was the pastor, and he made a comment that Senator Obama was in the audience. I leaned over to get a look and thought, "Oh yeah, that's the guy you said 'who?' about." But there he was with his wife, and the pastor made a comment, "Well, one day he might run for the president of the United States if his wife gives him permission." I kept thinking, "Who is this guy that would ask his wife's permission to run for the presidency of the United States?" It was like, "What manner of man is this?", and I thought, "Boy! That's interesting." There was no air of self-importance; no pretense. He was really a down-to-earth, ordinary kind of guy. In the back of your mind, you say, "This bears watching."

Then a couple of years later I am a bishop in Tennessee and Harold Ford, Jr. is running for Congress in a tight race, and of course it's a very controversial race because you have an African American running for this congressional seat. And we are political, social justice, civil rights activists, and we were supportive of his campaign. Senator Obama came to Tennessee to campaign for him. He came to Bethel AME church in Nashville, TN. He came that Sunday morning with Harold Ford, Jr. and he worshipped with us. And he was the same affable, smiling person. But there was an intensity about him that I did not see when I first met him in Chicago. My opinion at that moment was that he was focused on helping this candidate make it. We had conversation. He spoke at a rally near the stadium, and I remember listening to him and thinking, "There's more to him than a senator."

Meeting Barack Obama was sort of like when I first heard Bill Clinton speak. And everyone was saying Clinton is too young. He's not yet fifty. He's the governor of Arkansas. I remember going to hear Bill Clinton speak when I was in DC. I said, "I don't know what Bill Clinton those others are talking about, but this man makes sense. There's more to him than being what he is right now." And after I first heard Obama speak, I thought all in all there is more to him than being a senator. When the word got out that he was going to run for president, I thought in the back of my mind, "I guess Michelle gave him permission."

He ran, and, as I said, I knew there was more to him and more that he had to offer than where he was in the United States

Senate. Evidently the majority of the voters agreed, and they voted him in, not once but twice. Since that time, I have been more than impressed. Every now and then, in every generation, God sends us one or two people who have certain sets of gifts and skills to be able to handle things that ordinary people cannot handle. I don't know how Jackie Robinson could have played baseball and listened to all the manner of things they tossed at him and said to him. Yet he still hit home runs and played with superstar performance. I don't know how Martin Luther King did it. I don't know how Daisy Bates did it. She has got to be one of my most favorite people in the whole entire world. Although she could have been churning on the inside, she didn't break or crack. She walked to school, listening to all the people screaming and howling at her, demeaning her, intimidating her, threatening her. Yet she walked into that school house and was a good student. I don't know how many people would be able to do that.

As for President Obama, all manner of things have been said to him and done to him. Yet he still maintains poise, integrity, calm, and wisdom and is one of the best presidents we've had for the kinds of things that he has done. I believe this is the first president in years who has gone through the presidency without a scandal. There are no outside children. Kids aren't arrested for drugs or going off the deep end. Both he and Michelle are amazing. Anybody less than that would have gone off the deep end by now. When he gave the State of Union speech and the Congress member yelled, "You lie!", he just looked at him and gave him the side eye and kept right on going. He didn't miss a beat, because surely if he had responded, they would have blamed him and exonerated the man who had the nerve to inter-rupt the president of the United States in the middle of a State of the Union address. Who had ever heard of such a thing? I had never seen such disrespect to the Oval Office. Whether you like the president or not, you should never disrespect the office of the presidency.

Such awful treatment he received, but when you think about it, you have millions of people who now have healthcare insurance because of him. He has done what five presidents have not been able to do and that's to give universal healthcare to Americans. When I hear people say that Obamacare is terrible and is not going to do anything, I think about this guy driving me around at the Democratic Convention in Chicago who lost his wife because his insurance company had problems. I think about all the other people who could not get insurance because of a preexisting condition. And you pray that no one in your family or you are ever in a position where they may drop you.

But in spite of everything they have dumped on him, including the secret service misdoings, he has managed to raise the approval rating of the United States internationally. What he has done for women, not just the Ledbetter act, but appointing women to the Supreme Court—not because they were women but because they were qualified litigants—is big. He got us out of Iraq, which was his promise and he kept it. He also helped pull us out of Afghanistan. We are still there but at least it is downscaled.

What he has done for Historically Black Colleges and Universities has been great. I was in the Episcopal district where there is an HBCU that we have a responsibility to support. We still need more help to do that because the HBCU education process is still a valued entity. It is not an unnecessary thing, which a lot of people would like to say. People say, "Well, we don't need to have it now that we have integration." Yes, you do, but you have a lot of people who can't afford 40 and 50 thousand a year to go to school. You have those who are the first in their family and need the wraparound services that an HBCU will give a student if they are a first-generation or even second-generation college student.

AMEs have churches throughout the Caribbean. Bermuda, all throughout the Bahamas, we have AME churches all the way down to Guyana, which is the northern most part of South America that you can get. Thus we had churches in Cuba. And we never believed in our lifetime that there would be enough access to Cuba to see if we could find the remnants of the faith there, but President Barack Obama opened that door.

When former Vice President Al Gore was trying to highlight climate change and environmental issues, the people on the other side kept saying there's no such thing. This president came in and championed the greening of America and put in that climate change agenda all while you have an entire political party in the Senate and a whole Congress against him.

In spite of everything, he has respected the office. The office didn't make the man; he made the office. We had an opportunity as a country to celebrate our diversity and move into a post-racial society. But we drank the Kool-Aid and instead of celebrating our diversity we went back to the way it was. It's not that racism went away; it was just behind closed doors. His presidency just brought it out into the open. What was said behind closed doors and privately around dinner tables and at dinner parties was now being said out loud. And the fears and phobias that we may have thought to just be the opinion of a few, we found out there is a whole segment of the community that still feels this way. And so we find ourselves in the 21st century fighting again what our parents and grandparents had to fight for. Issues we thought were settled are not settled, and we still find ourselves in

America having to have laws to enforce diversity in a diversified country that is proud to say it is the melting pot of the world but that refuses to allow the melting to take place.

Bishop Vashti Murphy McKenzie is a bishop of the African Methodist Episcopal Church and currently serves as the presiding Prelate of the 10th Episcopal District.

LEADING WITH STRENGTH AND DIGNITY
by T. DeWitt Smith, Jr.

When I grew up in Chicago, it was never believed that an African-American would ever be elected to any higher office during our lifetime, let alone president of these United States. Now we know better. I first met our illustrious commander-in-chief in Washington, DC while serving as president of the Progressive National Baptist Convention in 2007 in a meeting called by Dr. Marian Wright-Edelman that was held in the Capitol. He came into the room as Senator Barack Obama. He was friendly, warm, and direct, promising Mrs. Edelman and us that he would work to secure the vote for over 9 million children who had no health or dental care. History knows he went beyond that to secure, by law, the Affordable Health Care Act for all Americans. Dr. Tyrone Pitts, who was serving as General Secretary, and I had been asked by Rev. Joshua DuBois to come on board and support the senator in his bid for the presidency. I promised to pray about it.

As the LORD convicted my heart to "get with the program," I yielded to the Holy Spirit and said to myself, "Why not!" A black man (biracial), born of a Kenyan father and a white mother, could in fact become the president of the United States of America. Some people I talked to argued that he needed to wait; many were looking forward to Senator Hillary Clinton becoming the nominee. We met with the senator from Illinois in Atlanta at Georgia Tech with a host of faith leaders, along with Dr. Joseph E. Lowery, President Emeritus of S.C.L.C. I walked over to shake his hand and repeated my name. Senator Obama said, "I know who you are, and my pastor, Rev. Otis Moss III, said to tell you hello. We had Easter dinner together last Sunday." We heard his speech to the crowd gathered there. He talked about change in America, chanting in sermonic style, "It's time to turn the page" and "Yes we can." Many of us at that moment felt that this was God's appointed man for our presidential future.

In our second meeting of the four historic African-American National Baptist Conventions in Atlanta, February 2008, I voiced in my sermon before a sea of several thousand black Baptists that so many black government representatives in Congress and in other elected federal, state, county, and municipal positions—especially those who were appointed to positions of responsibility—did not have to wait for their time. Why did Senator Obama have to wait? One month prior to the 2008 presidential election, Joshua DuBois and D. Paul Monteiro came to our PNBC Fall Leadership Conference and shared with our PNBC executive board and leaders present in Washington DC that I was the first of the national Baptist presidents to come forth and publicly support Senator Obama: they were now soliciting our vote. With support, prayer, and voting, Senator Barack H. Obama became our president: the first African-American to ascend to the highest civil office in our nation's history. What a history!

On election night, my wife, Aretta, Dr. Pitts, and I were in Chicago, close to the stage where he accepted the vote of the people of this country. We were later ushered into the tent where we personally greeted and congratulated President-elect and Mrs. Obama: history. The inauguration, though bone-chillingly cold, was heartwarming, seeing what "God had wrought": President Obama being sworn into leadership.

It was through the efforts of Dr. Pitts and Dr. Barbara Williams Skinner that I became co-chair with Dr. Barbara, forming the National African-American Clergy Network. Dr. Otis Moss, Jr. became our elder statesman and co-chair, along with Dr. Barbara and me. We were not to be disappointed; the historic African-American churches of every denomination, along with nonde-nominational leaders, came together to form a powerful coalition to secure the vote of the African-American and nonwhite faith groups across the nation. Once President Obama was elected, we focused our efforts in the National African-American Clergy Network (NAACN) on pushing for the Affordable Health Care Bill, which later became law.

This is a testimony to what coalitions of like-minded people can do to make things happen, with an understanding that God and government can work well even when religion and politics clash. (Politics and religion killed Jesus Christ—see my book *Drop the Rage, Turn the Page*).

With the assistance and influence of the faith community as we are called, we have seen our president succeed at almost everything Senator Mitch McConnell and the obstructionist right wing of the Republican Party have tried to block. They even tried to make him a one-term president. Thank God that didn't happen. President Obama has led the nation with strength and dignity. President and First Lady Michelle and the First Family have shown grace amidst negative criticism: a First Family worth emulating. President Obama's legacy includes helping our children get a sound college education by reducing debt; shaping public policy that became law; helping historic black colleges and universities; raising awareness about equity in pay for women to put them on a par with men on the same jobs; pushing for the minimum wage to rise, calling for implementation on the federal level; successfully dealing with Iran, domestic, and foreign policy; and putting Detroit and the automobile industry back on its feet. President Obama's life and leadership made history that cannot be erased. It will become his legacy on earth, even as it is in heaven, thank God Almighty.

Dr. T. DeWitt Smith, Jr. is Senior Pastor of Trinity Baptist Church of Metro Atlanta in Decatur, GA, and the co-chair of the National African-American Clergy Network.

PRESIDENT BARACK OBAMA:
THE PRIVILEGE OF A LIFETIME!

by Ambassador Suzan Johnson Cook

THE CONVENTION:

I was there for that moment in history. I remember, so well, the excitement in Denver at the 2008 Democratic Convention when the first African-American accepted the Democratic nomination for the Presidency of the United States. The Black clergy had met a few days earlier, and those who had been with Hillary sat with the faith advisors for Barack, and we became ONE in the SPIRIT. This was a moment in time, an Ecclesiastical Kairos moment, that demanded that we would Walk together, Talk together, Pray together, and Stay as ONE!

ELECTION DAY:
Then that November Election Day I was back home in Harlem when the roar erupted and folks were dancing in the streets, from the Apollo Theater to as far as the eye could see and the ear could hear as Barack Obama would be the president of the United States of America. OMG. This was what and who we had been waiting for: Strong, Black, Family intact, Brilliant, Resilient, Formidable, and Filled with Faith.

THE PHONE CALLS:
Then when I was asked on a phone call from the National African-American clergy advisory team to deliver one of the readings/prayers for the president on his first day in office, I leaped with joy—actually, "cried like a baby" is more accurately descriptive.

INAUGURATION DAY:
And then, with the coveted purple, gold, or orange passes, we rushed, trying to be as orderly as possible, but knowing that unless we moved strategically and quickly, we would miss the moment. We were held back for a few minutes, just as we were about to enter the area for our purple ticket pass holders and his motorcade went by. We caught a glimpse of OUR President. Cheering, Tearing, we were standing out in the cold, with pleasure and bated breath, for hours, as he took the oath of office on the steps that had been built with the hands of our slave ancestors. Every moment was a "WOW," "Thank you Jesus," "Praise God from whom all blessings flow," "We've come this far by faith" moment. Anyone we were near hugged us, and we hugged them. I was so glad to be sharing the moment with the three men in my life, my family: two African-American young men and one African-American dad, witnessing an African-American family getting ready to occupy the White House.

Our ancestors, who could not see or imagine this day, were there with us, in SPIRIT, as thousands upon thousands flew in by plane, rode in by train, bus, car service, or walked in through tunnels, or stood out on the mall, or sat near the stage, or stayed glued to the TV.

No one moved. Everyone around me was crying. And then, collectively, Blacks, Whites, Asians, Native Americans, Latinos, all around me, joined together and began to recite the Lord's prayer. Heaven was on earth, and earth was touching heaven. This was a pre-ordained, pre-determined, pre-anointed, Divinely-appointed and assigned moment in history.

GOD WAS UP TO SOMETHING:
Yes, he had run a great campaign, but there was something more happening. God was kissing us, and offering heavenly reparations for ALL the years of racism, neglect, rapes, rudeness, and insensitivity and inhumanity that we, as a people, had experienced.

THE WORSHIP SERVICE ON HIS FIRST DAY IN OFFICE:
At the CATHEDRAL, we robed and lined up, awaiting our instructions for rehearsal, when Joshua DuBois asked if we would mind taking a photo. Of course, we were thrilled to have been asked, and one by one all the program participants not only had the privilege of meeting and posing with President Obama and First Lady Michelle, but we were also joined by the Bidens and then later, in the sanctuary, entered the Clintons.

The service was the highlight of my life. I knew the Clintons personally, but I made eye contact with the First Lady as soon as she sat down. I KNEW everything was going to be all right—that America had, at its helm, the right man with the right woman and team for the job.

THE OTHER PHONE CALL:

There's so much to try to capsulize, but after the inaugural ball and other festivities ended, it was time to get to work. I was absolutely FLOORED to have received the phone call and nomination by Secretary of State Hillary Clinton, inviting me to join the Obama Administration. I was APPOINTED by President Barack H. Obama to be the first African-American and first woman to serve as the United States Ambassador at Large for International Religious Freedom, representing our president in more than 25 nations as his lead diplomat, attending and speaking at the United Nations General Assembly as the President's Ambassador and representing my parents: the late Wilbert T. and Dorothy C. Johnson, who started in the deep South as sharecroppers but who were able to escape the cruel fields and build wealth in America, as their family business still is the longest running Black-owned business in the Bronx, New York. I, their daughter, the descendant of those who had to use an outhouse, now could walk in the front door where a mighty man, President Barack Obama, lived in the WHITE HOUSE.

A PRIVILEGE:

I never forgot each day to thank God for my blessings. But on the days I was in the country, I walked past the White House each day and offered a prayer for the entire Obama family, by name. I also felt like one of his "Aarons and Hurs" to do such a good job in my role, that it would hold up his arms as he led our nation.

Systemic racism is deep and deeply entrenched in all of our systems, even government. And I heard and experienced some things, aimed at him, but received by whoever were his appointees, from the Senate confirmation hearings all the way through my tenure. But I would not waver nor sleep on my assignment.

For this was OUR president. What a privilege.

What a Mighty God we serve. Thank you, awesome God, for the Privilege to stand with BLACK ROYALTY and to serve our nation during his administration. May God Bless America!

Suzan Johnson Cook is a presidential advisor, pastor, theologian, author, activist, and academic who served as the United States Ambassador-at-Large for International Religious Freedom from April 2011 to October 2013.

AMERICA CHANGED FOREVER
by Rev. Dr. Wayne "Coach" Gordon

On November 4, 2008, America changed forever. I remember the day oh so well. After voting for Barack Obama, a person well known to us in the city of Chicago, I went home to relax and watch the election returns. My neighborhood of North Lawndale, an African-American community on Chicago's West Side, was very excited about the hope of Senator Obama becoming the 44th president of the United States.

When my wife, Anne, came home that night she was full of excitement and anticipation that Barack Obama might become our president. We had been invited to come to Grant Park in downtown Chicago, where soon-to-be President Obama would give his acceptance speech. I planned to watch it on TV and avoid the crowds, but Anne had other plans, as she wanted to be a part of this historic occasion. So we went, and I am so glad we did so.

We were with two African-American couples talking and waiting for Barack and Michelle Obama to come on stage. As we stood and waited, one of the men told me a story that has remained deeply implanted in my mind. He told Anne and me of his high school graduation speaker telling the entire graduating class that they could be anything they wanted to be, even president. When he got home, his father came into his room and sat on the side of his bed. "Son," he said, "you are a wonderfully talented young man and you can do great things, but the speaker misspoke." He went on to say, "You can do a lot of things, but you could never be the president of the United States because you are a black man." That night, with tears in all of our eyes, we rejoiced that we now had an African-American as our president.

President Obama has always been a person of kindness with gentle strength. He has handled himself as our president with grace and humility. I remember with fondness, before he was president, his being here with us at Lawndale Community Church. He took me aside and thanked me for all the work and sacrifices Anne, I, and our church had made to improve our community. He was so generous and caring with his words. What an encouragement this has been in our lives when we have gone through hard times.

Clearly one of the great legacies of the Barack Obama presidency has been his devotion to family. He has exemplified a loving husband and devoted father his entire eight years. Anne and I, along with our son Austin, were invited to Washington, D.C. to be with the president when he set forth his Father's Initiative of helping fathers be more involved in their children's lives. We were on the stage with him and placed right behind him, so when pictures were taken the three of us were in them. When the President walked by, he waved, said hi, and shook Austin's hand. That was a special time for us.

President Barack Obama built a wonderful sense of good will in the world. On a recent trip to Kenya, I showed the children of

Kibera, Africa's largest slum, a picture of me with the president. The Kenyan children all cheered with great enthusiasm. They love President Barack Obama and, because of that, they love America.

The world will miss our 44th president, as he faithfully served all of America and the world with love, grace, humility, and compassion.

Rev. Dr. Wayne "Coach" Gordon is Pastor of Lawndale Community Church in Chicago.

THERE IS SOMETHING ABOUT THIS MAN...
The Anointing and the Appointing of President Barack Obama
by Rev. Dr. George E. Holmes

All the statistics in the world cannot measure President Barack Hussein Obama's greatness appropriately. How can they, when he was chosen by God for this moment? Things and people just don't line up like that, unless God is involved! There is something about this MAN, which is beyond the imagination! No disrespect, but he is too cool. His swag is too on point...his walk, his talk, his processing, his demeanor, his mannerisms. He didn't get here overnight, he got here over time. Centuries that is! He was prayed into existence. He fits right into 2 cultures, with parents of 2 different races and he understands and masters both races and cultures. Therefore, when the economic crisis happened, he was tailor-made for the job for which he was pur-posed by God. Any other time in U.S. history, President Obama may not have been. Things were orchestrated in a way that set him up to be President. From President Bill Clinton, to the election loss of 2000 of Vice President Al Gore, to the presidency of President George W. Bush and to virtually out of nowhere the presidency of Barack Obama. He defied the conventional process, the way it is usually done through protocol. I have one word that many believers are very familiar with: God! Nobody but God could have orchestrated these sets of circumstances like this! He was destined to be President of the United States of America. Undeniably he has proven, that his presidency is bigger than one can imagine. He has Divine favor.

He was born to play chess not checkers. His strategies, not his feelings, are ahead of others. He operates in systems; he operates in principles, which guide his individual decisions. These governing principles were set up before he became President. He operates within those systems. He has principles that govern his thoughts from how he reflects, to how he answers, to how he controls his emotions. He was able to work in the system but not be 'of' the system. Because he understood the system. As the millennials would say, ‹President Obama wasn't new to this, he grew to this›. But in order to get to, he had to go through.

I know all of this because I had a front row seat to one of the greatest administrations of any President or any King of all time. I was hand chosen by God to assist one of the greatest leaders in all of history. I am not saying this because he is black, but he is; or because he is a black man, but he is; or because I am a black man, but I am. I am saying this because I was born to give him what I could. I am saying this not because of a condition, but my position, that allowed me to see the condition, of his position, as President of the United States of America. There are very few people who have been in and out of the White House, during the 8 years of the Obama Presidency more than I.

Allow me to share my perspective, from a place of humility to a place of privilege.

Dating back to 2006, I was selected by the Mayor of the District of Columbia to be the Chairperson of the Mayor's Transition Religious Affairs Committee for the District of Columbia. I completed my assignment with excellence as I recruited, organized, compiled and presented to the Democratic Mayor and his Senior Administration, a 2007 Mayoral Executive Summary Report of my findings and recommendations. In 2008, I was commissioned by the Executive Director of DC for Obama to be the Faith Coordinator for then-Senator, Democratic Nominee for President of the United States, Barack Obama. I took on this assignment with the same kind of excellence I demonstrated before, however, something was a little different. There was a spiritual presence that was over me. I could see Divine intervention. God's Hand was in motion. I was working around the clock, even in the early hours of the morning. I asked myself, "Why am I working this hard for Senator Obama"? The answer was soon revealed: the Spirit of the Lord was on him. I could see God's Anointing as God was ordering his steps. And I went back to work. And boy did we work!

From the literature dissemination of "Called to Christ: Barack Obama's Testimony and Senator Barack Obama Called to Serve", to the Get Out to Vote (GOTV) in the Faith Community, to the 'Yes, We Can and a Barack Obama Get Out to Vote Sunday', the work was relentless. I organized many conference calls wherein candidate Obama and various leaders e.g., Oprah Winfrey, Congressman James Clyburn, Governor Deval Patrick of Massachusetts and Sean 'Diddy' Combs discussed his vision for Change, with assigned Clergy praying for his vision to reach fruition. We assembled leadership throughout the Washington Metropolitan Area in concert with countless of others throughout the Nation, and as a result, Barack Hussein Obama was elected the 44th President of the United States of America!

November 4th, 2008 changed everything. After Election Day, I received the phone call. The President Elect's Transition Team asked me where the Obamas should worship on the Sunday prior to the Inauguration. I vetted discreetly with a few others, and while there were many suitable Places of Worship, I suggested the historic Nineteenth Street Baptist Church in Washington, DC. On Sunday, January 18th the Nineteenth Street Baptist Church welcomed the Obamas. I further suggested St. John's Episcopal Church, where the Obamas worshipped on Inauguration Day, while also compiling the list of Clergy Leaders who participated in this historic worship celebration. On Wednesday, January 21st, 2009 on the final Inauguration Worship Service, President Obama attended the National Prayer Service at Washington National Cathedral along with a host of Faith Leaders that I recommended. Also, in between were the Presidential Inaugural swearing-in tickets, Presidential Inaugural Balls and President Obama's call for a National Day of Service.

From there this newly elected president and his administration were hard at work. They were moving at warp speed to get this Nation back on course. His appointed Executive Director of the White House Office of Faith-Based and Neighborhood Partnerships and the White House Public Liaison for Religious Affairs, were transparent on the urgent mission of President Obama. They included the newly organized Obama National African American Clergy Leadership Working Group into many aspects of the Obama Administration.

President Obama was consumed with rebuilding our Nation. And work the President did! He rolled up his sleeves and got busy. If you had a suggestion that could make this Country better, the President was listening. We had weekly calls and frequent meetings from discussions concerning: the President's Recovery Plan, Department of Education, Veterans Affairs, Energy and Climate, Business Sunday, Poverty and Serving Marginalized Communities, White House Domestic Policy Council, Office of Management and Budget, Rural Issues and Agricultural Programs, U.S. Government Haiti Earthquake Disaster Response, HUD Secretary, BP Oil Spill, Fannie Mae and Freddie Mac on the Making Home Affordable Plan, Criminal Justice Reform, National Service Legislation, Department of Homeland Security, America›s Children Report, Women's History Month, Corporate, the Impact of a Government Shutdown, Pathways to Opportunity, Department of Treasury, Department of Commerce, FEMA / HSEMA on Preparedness, Service America Act, Corporation for National and Community Service, White House Health Care Summit, First Lady's Let's Move Initiative, Community College Initiative, HBCUs, EPA Secretary, Transparency in Government, My Brothers' Keeper Initiative, Department of Labor Secretary, Small Business Administration, White House African Summit, Unemployment Insurance Extension, Department of Transportation, CBC, Seniors, Social Security, Immigration Reform, Credit Cardholders› Bill of Rights, USAID, Homelessness, Federal Budget, HHS Secretary, Issues concerning the Faith Community, Department of Justice, Affordable Health Care Act, Foreign Diplomacy, Hurricane Katrina, Job Creation, Office of Social Innovation and Civic Participation, United Nations, President's Obama's Service Agendas, President's Supreme Court Justices and Nominees and President Obama's acceptance of the Nobel Peace Prize, to name a few.

Within months of President Obama's new Administration came the idea to honor and officially welcome to the Nation's Capital the President's Religious Appointees, Executive Director of the White House Office of Faith-Based and Neighborhood Partnerships, Rev. Joshua DuBois and White House Public Liaison for Religious Affairs, Mr. Paul Monteiro. This *"Welcome to DC Reception"* was held at the Washington, DC's Executive Office Branch, the Historic John A. Wilson District Building. The Mayor's Office, DC City Council, and I architected and organized one of the largest political and religious receptions ever held, with hundreds upon hundreds of Interfaith, Neighborhood and Business Leaders in attendance within the Halls of Government.

Surely, some of us attended White House Easter Prayer Breakfasts, White House Christmas Receptions, the White House Champions of Change, White House Council of Economic Advisers, White House Stakeholders Policy Meetings, Presidential Historic Signings, National Day of Prayer and White House Briefings with National Leaders with the President and the Senior Administration. There were weekly White House Big Table Meetings, the White House Meeting with African American Clergy Leaders and Senior Advisor to the President, Valerie Jarrett and visits with the President and First Lady Mrs. Michelle Obama hosting foreign dignitaries and diplomats. However, the one thing I am going to miss most about this phenomenal President is his God given ability to take young people's hopes and dreams, and those that were disenfranchised and make those hopes and dreams his own. What 'Audacity of Hope' he has!

In closing, President Barack Hussein Obama will live on in the annals of history and on the pages of time. Songs will be sung about him. Books will be written. Streets will be named. I don't know where or when it was in his life that he fully accepted his calling, but I think he demonstrated to many of us, that we should fully accept each of our callings, in our own lives. As this Holy Scripture spoke to President Obama through the echoes of time, let us follow likewise from Hebrews 12:1, "Wherefore seeing we also are compassed about with so great a cloud of witnesses, let us lay aside every weight, and the sin which doth so easily beset us, and let us run with patience the race that is set before us."

President Obama, as in the words of the late great Rev. Dr. Martin Luther King, Jr., "An individual has not started living until he can rise above the narrow confines of his individualistic concerns to the broader concerns of all humanity." Thank you for answering your call to serve all humanity. Your life has truly inspired and transformed the nations of the world. The world will be forever changed. Thank you, President Obama, for your invaluable service and contributions to the United States of America. I am humbled and honored to have had the privilege of seeing you up close and personal. Well done, Mr. President, Well done!

Rev. Dr. George E. Holmes, M.A., MDiv., President Obama National Clergy Leadership Group

PEOPLE MATTER

by Roy Medley

President Obama's eight years of service can be summed up in my perspective in two words: "People matter."

My first encounter with him was as then-candidate Obama. His campaign had been regularly scheduling listening sessions across the country with different constituencies. My invitation was to attend a gathering of evangelical leaders. I went with mixed emotions, always cautious with political overtures because I did not want either my office (General Secretary, American Baptist Churches) or me to be used in a partisan way as a campaign tool.

We gathered in a conference room—around 30 of us if I remember correctly—and he listened. He listened to the various concerns voiced around the table about policy on matters such as abortion, domestic poverty, violence, and education, and when he engaged us with responses or probed an issue with follow-up questions, it was always with respect and genuine interest in our perspectives and positions. This was not the easiest audience for him. There were clearly differences on key issues, as well as places where his and our concerns converged. But he listened and welcomed the give and take as he sought to take the pulse of this group of religious leaders. My take away from that event was that all persons genuinely mattered to him.

During these past eight years, I have had other occasions to be with President Obama, his staff, and members of his administration in addition to following news coverage of him. Over these eight years he struggled to right a tanking economy and save jobs in the midst of an international meltdown; he responded to the increasing instances of gun-related massacres; he led against increasingly emboldened racism; he countered Islamaphobia and attacks on religious liberty; he ordered torture to be ended as contrary to American values; he championed healthcare as a right and not a privilege; he fought to secure the civil rights of all. In all this, it was clear that he was guided by the core conviction that people matter – even those who disagreed with him and vilified him.

Many of us will never forget the night of his first election and the turnout of folks of every race, culture, and religious background to celebrate this seeming turning point in American history that was opening a door to a more just and compassionate society. Those hopes were quickly dashed by the virulent political attacks upon him, by gridlocked partisanship in Washington, by increased efforts to curtail voting and other rights, by the increasing economic divide between rich and poor, and by the fear of terrorism.

President Obama, however, persevered with courage and compassion. Whether it was serving as Consoler-in-Chief to a nation reeling from the Sandy Hook massacre or the murder of Trayvon Martin and other men of color; whether it was continuing to champion immigration, tax, and prison reform; whether it was visiting Flint, Michigan in the wake of lead tainting the city water supply through the malfeasance of government officials or saving the jobs of autoworkers in hard-hit Detroit; whether seeking to build international coalitions to counter terrorism or bridging the divide between black and blue lives; President Obama has championed the call that all people matter and that the goal of the common good is the highest good to which we can devote our energies as a people.

Rev. Dr. A. Roy Medley is General Secretary Emeritus of the American Baptist Churches.

THE POLITICS OF RACE

BARACK OBAMA: A PROFILE IN COURAGE

by David A. Renwick

I well remember my wife returning home from the public school where she taught on November 4, 2008, the day when President Obama was first elected. One of her many black colleagues, Cynthia, had shared with her not only her own joy at being able to vote for a black candidate for the presidency, but also the deep and painful concern of her mother, who found herself unable to vote, paralyzed by the fear that once Mr. Obama became president someone would take his life simply because he was black. Earlier in the campaign, when Mr. Obama himself was asked about this fear, he responded by acknowledging that while his family and friends were concerned about his safety, his own situation was insignificant compared to that of Dr. King: "He didn't have Secret Service protection. I can't even comprehend the degree of courage that was required, and look what he did."

In this comment, published in *USA Today*, Mr. Obama downplayed his courage. Most courageous people do. They tend to focus on what needs to be done and then get on with it, without thinking of their actions as in any way virtuous. But in seeking and standing for office, I believe that Mr. Obama's courage cannot and must not be underestimated. Nor must his courage be underestimated in the way that he has exercised the office regarding issues of race over the last four years of his presidency since the shooting of Trayvon Martin in 2012.

From 2012 to 2016, multiple shootings of black men and boys (especially but not only by police: think Charleston as well as Ferguson) have highlighted the ongoing issue of racism in our nation. Fundamental to the Christian faith are two truths that should make racism, for Christians at least, unacceptable: the creation of all human beings in the image of God (Genesis

1:26) and the redemption of all human beings by the love of God, seen especially in the death of Jesus: a death for all (John 3:15, 2 Corinthians 5:15). In his recent book, *The End of White Christian America* (Simon & Schuster, 2016), Robert P. Jones highlights the distance that separates the church – both white and black – from this ideal and the obliviousness of many whites (Christian and non-Christian) to the fact that there is a problem at all. On the other hand, one of the criticisms leveled against Mr. Obama from within the African-American community is that he has simply not done enough to bring institutional and legal power to bear on the situation. (See, for example, Georgetown University professor Michael Eric Dyson's article, "Barack Obama, the President of Black America? What the haters and the hagiographers get wrong" (*New York Times*, June 24, 2016). The simple fact of an African-American presidency has clearly not eradicated racism, whether in personal or systemic forms. Who can argue against this? More can always be done!

However, what I would argue is that President Obama has played his cards just about right. In the end, the lasting legacy of his presidency surely lies not just on the level of particular policy agreements, disagreements, and changes, but rather with *Mr. Obama's ability as someone of a particular and clear ethnic identity to be the president of all within our nation while not in any way diminishing his own identity or diminishing the seriousness of unresolved issues relating to race.* This involves standing up to cries from both white and black. It involves being visibly comfortable with his own racial identity. It involves letting the whole nation know that there's much more work to be done. This is not easy. It's a fine line. In fact, it takes both wisdom and a great deal of courage. But this is what I've seen in Mr. Obama.

David A. Renwick is Senior Pastor at The National Presbyterian Church in Washington, DC.

A REFLECTION OF RACE, RACIAL TENSION & POLICING ISSUES IN AMERICA

by Dr. Natalie A. Francisco

There is a cancer that is slowly destroying our nation in the form of unjust laws and practices that stem from the roots of our country's past sins. From these roots have sprung weeds of racial tension, cultural insensitivity, and the tragic loss of life from the times of slavery to the unnecessary recent killings of Terence Crutcher in Tulsa, OK; Keith Lamont Scott in Charlotte, NC; Alton Sterling in Baton Rouge, LA; and Philando Castille in Falcon Heights, MN. Then there was the shooting of 12 police officers (5 of whom died) in Dallas, TX; and countless other victims whose tragic deaths have garnered national media attention—Trayvon Martin, Eric Garner, Michael Brown, John Crawford III, Tamir Rice, Freddie Gray, Sandra Bland, and others. Race, racial tension, and policing are but a few of the myriad of prevailing issues that our nation's 44th President, Barack Hussein Obama, had to confront with concern and candor to be understood and addressed from the perspective of our nation's first African-American commander-in-chief.

In an article by NPR White House correspondent Scott Horsley titled "Obama Walks Fine Line on Race and Policing," some of President Obama's comments regarding racial tension and policing are underscored in the aftermath of too many senseless deaths. Whereas the President reiterated that the majority of our nation's police officers are doing a good job in their quest to protect and serve, he stated that "the law too often feels as if it is being applied in discriminatory fashion. These are real issues, and we have to lift them up and not deny them or try to tamp them down...And when incidents like this occur, there's a big chunk of our fellow citizenry that feels as if because of the color of their skin, they are not being treated the same. And it hurts. And that should trouble all of us."

There is a reason for the anger and unrest that exists across America. Many want to do something, but don't know what to do. Crowds of concerned citizens are rallying together in city streets across the nation with nonviolent, peaceful protests to emphasize and support the Black Lives Matter movement. Others are meeting behind the scenes to devise and implement strategies to address the inequities that have prevailed due to systemic racism that is both covert and overt in policies and practices. Systemic racism and bigotry must be addressed by those who aren't afraid to speak truth to power wherever and whenever necessary, whether in our families, friendships, churches, workplaces, or other institutions. Our voices must be heard in our judicial, legislative, and executive branches of government. We must continue to pray for the families of victims as well as for the protection of our own families. However, it is also important for us to be informed and aware of what is happening around us as well as to us as people of color. It is just as important to get to know our city council, school board members, mayor, judges, state representatives, senators, congresspersons, and governors, and to know the platforms and issues they stand for and whether they address the needs in our own communities. We must let our voices be heard by voting our conscience to elect our president of choice. That is exactly how President Barack Obama was able to successfully serve two terms in the White House--by the majority vote and will of the American people.

Obama's presidency has not been an easy one, given the conflagration of domestic and foreign issues vying for his attention. Many may have unrealistically believed that racial tensions and policing issues would be immediately resolved because there was finally an African-American president who could identify with and address issues that people of color face daily. The truth of the matter is that race, racial tension, and policing issues have been, are, and will remain on the social consciousness of our nation and its people. Although we are grateful for the initiation and work of the President's Task Force on 21st Century Policing, it is obvious that no one president can address these issues. All of us must take personal responsibility for our own actions (without allowing anger to escalate) by responding intelligently and proactively to pervading issues that confront our communities. We must do so as concerned citizens, community and church leaders, police officers, and criminal justice and government officials conscientiously working together to build relationships of mutual respect, trust, and accountability.

Dr. Natalie A. Francisco is a co-pastor of Calvary Community Church in Hampton, VA and Founder/Executive Director of Women of Worth & Worship, LLC.

A SALUTE TO PRESIDENT BARACK H. OBAMA
by Dr. James C. Perkins

Our eyes shed tears. Our hearts were filled with joy. We looked on in disbelief as it became evident that Senator Barack Hussein Obama of Illinois would become the 44th president of the United States of America.

This election had special significance because Mr. Obama became, in fact, the first African-American president of this nation. It seemed like an impossible dream. Even if Mr. Obama had been a household name at the time of his candidacy, it would still have seemed like an exercise in futility. As it was, most of us had hardly heard of him.

He had not been on the national stage or involved in national politics for a long period of time. Many of us asked each other and ourselves, *Why is this brother running for president? This country will never elect a black man as president. And besides, nobody knows him. Plus, he's got the wrong name!*

Yet as the campaign progressed and we heard him give those powerful speeches and then saw the polls in Iowa and New Hampshire give him favorable numbers, we began to think that what at the outset seemed impossible might not be so unrealistic and impossible after all! That "rooting for the underdog" spirit kicked in, and suddenly all of us felt we had a personal stake in this election like never before. This was a dream that our foremothers and forefathers could never have conceived.

There was a brief period after the election when we began to think that maybe this country wasn't as racist as we had thought. There was a lot of chatter about this nation having evolved into a post-racial society. We thought that just possibly the election of Mr. Obama as the nation's first African-American president meant the end of racism. We thought all the high platitudes were true: "You can be anything you want to be. No more excuses for not achieving your dream. It's no longer the color of your skin that matters. It's your ability and the content of your character that matter most."

But all this dreamy idealistic thinking notwithstanding, we were not totally shocked when on Inauguration Day, a group of Republican Congressmen announced that their political agenda was to see that Obama would be a one-term president. From that moment, no matter how he tried to reach across the aisle and work with others on behalf of the advancement of the country, they simply would not cooperate.

He inherited the worst economy this nation had faced since the Great Depression of the 1930s. He proposed stimulus dollars to jumpstart the economy. They opposed that! He wanted the federal government to invest in rebuilding our crumbling infrastructure and create jobs in the process. They opposed that!

They did their best to oppose everything he proposed in order to make him look like his was a failed presidency. And all of it was not just a matter of partisan politics. It was because he is a black man! What if they had worked with him? How different might this country be now?

So much for a post-racial society. So much for the end of racism. The election of President Obama generated a resurgence of racism in the country the likes of which we have not experienced since the 1960s. While for some the election of a black man as president meant progress for the nation, for others it was a sign that the nation was deteriorating, and groups arose chanting, "I want my country back!" By implication, they still want an America where all persons are not considered equal. Some still want a nation where segregation and discrimination are the law of the land.

Despite the efforts of Republicans, President Obama did save the economy. He saved the car industry from total collapse and the thousands of jobs that were in jeopardy. His policies created millions of new jobs, so as he leaves office after his second term, he proudly leaves us with the lowest unemployment rate we have had in a number of years.

Despite the efforts of the Republicans, President Obama gave us the Affordable Health Care Act, providing 20 million people with health care they could not otherwise afford. This is a monumental achievement given the fact that this nation has been trying to pass a healthcare bill going all the way back to the presidency of Theodore Roosevelt.

And this is to mention only a few of his stellar achievements. After a successful second term in office, he leaves with a popularity rating of over 50 percent!

We thank President Obama for being the great man that he is. He is cool under pressure. Everything he does, he does at the level of excellence. He is a wonderful role model, a wonderful husband, father, and family man. He is a smart and shrewd politician.

He is this nation's first African-American president, but he will not be the last. There is an eight-year-old boy or girl out there somewhere who doesn't know what it means at this point to have a white president. Their dream has been set. Their ambition has been fired. And they're saying within themselves, "I want to be the president of the United States." And they will figure out how to do it. The template has been set, thanks to President Obama.

At some point in this nation's history, race will not matter as much as it does now. The world has become a global community. In the future, ability and character will matter more than the color of one's skin. In that sense, President Obama has become the template for the leader of the future.

HAIL TO THE CHIEF! MAY GOD BLESS YOU WITH HEALTH, STRENGTH, LONG LIFE, AND MANY MORE YEARS OF SERVICE TO GOD, YOUR NATION, AND FELLOW PERSONS!

Dr. James C. Perkins serves as the pastor of Greater Christ Baptist Church in Detroit, MI. Also, he currently serves as the president of the Progressive National Baptist Convention, Inc.

Mr. President

A REFLECTION ON THE PRESIDENCY OF BARACK OBAMA

by Dr. Keith W. Byrd, Sr.

In January 2008 the unimaginable happened— a Black man named Barrack Hussein Obama was inaugurated as the 44th president of the United States of America. This amazing feat was only surpassed by his second inaugural in January 2012. Many in our country, particularly in the African-American community, never thought this was possible and certainly not in our lifetimes. Yet it happened, and it has left a lasting and impactful reality on the nation.

As I reflect on the Obama presidency, now that the sun has set upon it, there are numerous social, economic, and political achievements that can and should be celebrated. Perhaps his most visible and groundbreaking social achievement in terms of policy is the Affordable Care Act, better known as Obamacare. Through this landmark legislation, more than 20 million Americans who were previously uninsured and in many instances uninsurable now have access to healthcare for themselves and their families. As controversial as this legislation and subsequent law has been for some, by all measures it is a massive accomplishment. Economically, the Obama Administration achieved tremendous success through instituting policies and measures that led to one of the greatest economic recoveries in our nation's history.

In eight years, President Obama guided and presided over an economy that produced millions of new jobs, stabilized and strengthened markets nationally and internationally, and restored America's standing as an economic superpower. Politically, President Obama has revolutionized the way in which national campaigns are conducted. The political landscape has forever been altered due to his tremendous ability to organize communities and mobilize voters utilizing social media. In addition, President Obama and his team were successful in changing the electoral map through two presidential campaign cycles, building on what has come to be known as the Obama Coalition.

While all of the aforementioned achievements and many others too numerous to mention here are laudable and rather tempting to expound upon in this reflection, I want to suggest that the most impactful reality of the Obama presidency may not be directly attributable to President Obama nor to any specific initiatives, policies, or legislation produced by his administration. Perhaps the most impactful reality of the Obama presidency is the exposing of the deep social divisions that persist in America. These social divisions are primarily centered around race, education, and economics. While many sociologists have suggested to us that we live in a post-racial America, the reality appears to be to the contrary. Much of the angst and frustration that has been stirred and manifested in raucous rallies across the country, particularly Trump rallies during the current presidential campaign, has largely been in response to eight years of having a Black president. It has been well documented throughout American history that whenever there have been economic challenges, racial tensions seemed to increase particularly between whites and Blacks. In this instance, that racial tension has been even greater because a Black man was in the White House.

An even deeper look at these social divisions that have been exposed during the Obama presidency suggests that not only are they racial but they are also based on educational and economic disparities. While the majority population in America is still Caucasian, minorities are disproportionately impacted by the educational and economic disparities that persist. Yet we continue to see backlash or "whitelash" against minorities that I believe is the direct result of the Obama presidency. We must not back away from the reality that the rise of Trump as a presidential possibility was largely facilitated by the intense and intentional focus on the persistent social divisions prevalent in America that were more evidently manifested in the person of Barrack Hussein Obama. However successful this tactic may have proven to be for some, it threatens to undermine the very core of America's chief confession, "We the People." It is not "we the white people", "we the wealthy people", "we the educated people", but rather "WE" as in all of the people, regardless of social, political, or economic status.

As a result of this tactical undermining, it appears that the greatest challenge facing the newly-elected president will be to somehow unite the country while simultaneously addressing the social divisions that have reemerged with greater intensity due in large measure to the presidency of the first African-American president. What we may have thought was dead and buried we now know is not only alive but doing quite well. If God is to continue to bless America, we must humble ourselves, turn from our wicked ways, and seek God's face. Then and only then will He bring healing to this land.

Dr. Keith Byrd is the senior pastor of Zion Baptist Church of Washington, DC.

Mr. President

NEVER PROUDER TO BE AN AMERICAN
by Steve Park

I remember, at age 7 living in South Korea, imagining what this mythical place called America was like as our family prepared to emigrate there. On our black and white TV with rabbit ear antennas, I remember watching "Sesame Street" and "The Brady Bunch," thinking that America must be the most amazing place ever conceived.

I also remember moving to Houston at that age, and I remember the first time being called a "chink" at school and having to endure strangers telling our family as we were about to walk into a restaurant to "go back to China," even though of course none of us had ever been there. I came of age during the '80s and grew cynical about our racialized culture; I remember thinking as an adolescent that no person of color would ever be president in my lifetime.

The first time I had even heard of Barack Obama was listening to him speak at the Democratic Convention in 2004. I was immediately drawn to his visionary and inspirational speech. Somehow, he was speaking in a way that resonated with me and, I believe, to my generation.

When Barack Obama made the decision to run for president in 2007, I had my doubts. Is the United States ready for a black president? Would they actually vote for a president of color? And he's even got a funny sounding name! I shed some tears on election night in 2008 when Obama was declared the winner. I remember the hope I felt as I lifted my hands in the air at the announcement and hugged my wife. As a Korean-American, I have never been prouder to be an American nor prouder of America than I was that night.

Today, I'm so thankful that President Obama had the faith that I did not have. I'm so thankful for my children, who are now 11 and 13 and who never have to wonder if a person of color can be president. For them, Barack Obama is the only president they have known firsthand; they will have to adjust to seeing a white President in the White House.

As a Korean-American, it's hard for me to imagine the burden President Obama has had to carry as the first president of color in our nation's history. He has had to endure racist attacks, people who have tried to delegitimize his presidency, and even animosity toward his family. Yet he has handled his role with tremendous grace and class and served without scandal. Our nation truly owes him and his family a debt.

I live in Washington, DC, in a historic black neighborhood, Anacostia. I work and minister among African-Americans living in public housing just 12 blocks from the US Capitol. Our nation has a long way to go in dealing with its legacy of racism and its issues of poverty and social justice, but I will be forever grateful for the presidency of Barack Obama, for both me and my family and for all people of color in our nation.

Steve Park is the Executive Director at Little Lights Urban Ministries in Washington, DC.

THE OBAMA IMPACT
by Dr. Lisa Weah

He was the first U.S. President who truly understood the experience of being black in America. Never again would little black children where I pastor in Baltimore City give "cute" school speeches about one day becoming president of the United States to the indulgent applause of adults who celebrate their fanciful imaginations and creative writing skills.

We joyously cried along with the Rev. Jesse Jackson on that historic election night, and even more with Rep. John Lewis on that historic Inauguration Day, as we watched Barack Hussein Obama raise his right hand on the steps of our U.S. Capitol. Oh, how far we thought our country had come! Split shot photos of President Obama and the Rev. Dr. Martin Luther King, Jr. immediately hit social media. We could not have imagined at that moment how dramatically the next eight years would expose the ugly duality of our "Two Americas."

Born in the immediate aftermath of the Civil Rights movement, I had never seen a "colored only" sign, nor sat in the rear of a bus. In fact, I was a second-generation, college-educated, middle class professional who was only vaguely familiar with public transportation, until June of 2008. That was when I was elected pastor of the New Bethlehem Baptist Church in the Sandtown-Winchester community of West Baltimore.

By my first pastoral anniversary, only months into the Obama presidency, I had made two startling discoveries: 1) there were "Two Americas," and 2) seminary could never have fully prepared me for my new assignment. We were proudly watching our First Daughters— our First *Black* Daughters— wake up each morning in a house "built by slaves" (FLOTUS). Yet I was driving daily into a community that 2016 presidential candidate Bernie Sanders would later describe as akin to a "third world country less than an hour from our nation's capital!"

But when the Obamas took up residence at 1600 Pennsylvania Ave, the mask came off. America's ugly "isms" and phobias were all exposed: racism, classism, sexism, homophobia, and on and on. The hashtag protests began, and the body count was on the rise. We were painfully watching (thanks to cell phone cameras) what America never wanted uncovered— and was ashamed, or so we thought, for the world to see.

I will forever remember Palm Sunday of 2015 and the summer that followed. As we turned the corner into the end of the second Obama presidential term, I exited my church after service to hear that one of our young neighbors had died from injuries sustained the previous Sunday while being taken into police custody. Our neighbor's name was Freddie Gray. I did not know Freddie, but I had met and gotten to know many "Freddies" since becoming pastor of NBBC in 2008. I met his family, and I have met many other families with similar stories since then. I watched my beloved president talk personally with each of them after a D.C. Town Hall meeting a year later. That the leader of the free world would make time in his schedule to show genuine compassion and concern to some of his most socially disinherited constituents generated a climate of change in these underserved communities. Our concerns were validated; our leaders cared— not just on the surface by issuing statements from a podium afar, but by meeting us where we were, looking us directly in the eye, and personally articulating outrage, sorrow, and resolve.

Sandtown also began to change; relationships between and among people, police, politicians, and pastors were being repaired. Systems and policies that had long been faulty and ineffective were being exposed and addressed. Eyes began looking past the surface— the empty dilapidated houses, corner liquor stores, and "street thugs" — and seeing the hearts, hopes, and dreams of the people who called this place home.

President Obama's leadership has ushered in much-needed consideration of and attention to many of the problems in our urban communities. Despite the fact that the president-elect has made it his ambition to remove all traces of President Obama's time in office, his legacy will be broad and deep— broad because it impacted the minds and hearts of *all* people to come together for the greater good; deep because when those little black children give speeches about becoming president of the United States, they'll now have proof that it is, indeed, possible.

President Obama's legacy is one of grace, honor, and strength. Only history will tell how the true impact of his presidency affected change in our urban communities.

Dr. Lisa M. Weah is Senior Pastor of the New Bethlehem Baptist Church in Baltimore, MD.

"YES, WE CAN!"
by Dr. Jamal H. Bryant

"So do not throw away your confidence." (Hebrews 10:35a)

The presidency of Barack Hussein Obama represents a first in American history. It is a signature event in the history of the African Diaspora as well as an epiphany in the faith formation of the oppressed.

In believing God, there has always been an amalgam of "nevertheless," "anyhow," and a "suddenly" to inspire us to look for that which must come. Surely we have seen faith prescribe the very essence of what we need while in the midst of the agony of protracted waiting. African-American believers in every generation have ascribed to the God of the Red Sea Deliverance and the God of the Fiery Furnace Deliverance with a glorious and prophetic praise for our "breakthrough" deliverance. This victory has released itself time and time again throughout the generations, and yet it is one that quite necessarily remains supernaturally "at hand." We still embody the hope that is fortified from every "nevertheless" until we actualize each victory.

From the perspective of our belief, the pardon of every Barabbas, the hypocrisy of every Pilate, the strategic betrayal of every Judas, and the sorrow of every Mary prepared the way in the Spirit realm for the inauguration of the Obamas. This is not a conundrum when time revealed attaches itself to civilizations, generations, and communities defined by human occupation and eternal destiny. Centuries of a historic pathway become clear when we connect the dots. We are here, and there can be no resurrection of this nation apart from an authentic repentance. The miracle of the Obamas to our nation is confronted with the continued idolatry of Eurocentric people.

The Obamas' Black presence in the White House unleashed the subterranean racism in America to apocalyptic proportions from the hallowed halls of Congress to the camps of the most reactionary "off the grid" white nationalists. The presidency of Barack Hussein Obama has not spared African-Americans the scourge of racial hatred that has permeated every aspect of American history and culture. Even attaining the highest office in the land did not immunize him from the sting of eight years of obstructionism organized by the Republican Party in the Congress and the Senate.

So demonic is the stronghold of racism in America!

Nevertheless, we as a people, Believe GOD.

Abandoned by fundamentalist evangelical white church leaders, We Believe GOD.

Traumatized by the overt, unmerited violence and death perpetrated by the badge and the robe in the judicial system, We Believe GOD.

Isolated from recovery opportunities for addiction that are based on zip codes, We Believe GOD.

Looking into the future through the lens of faith, We Believe GOD.

We "decree and declare":

YES WE CAN believe in the grace and capacity of GOD to defy the structure and intergenerational impact of systemic racism in America.

YES WE CAN withstand the forces of misinformation and the proselytism of ubiquitous hatred and violence in America.

YES WE CAN summon the inner fortitude, discipline, and compassion to participate in this imperfect democracy until America is transformed into a nation of "liberty and justice for all."

Dr. Jamal Harrison Bryant is Senior Pastor of the Empowerment Temple AME Church in Baltimore, MD.

RACE CONSCIOUSNESS AFTER PRESIDENT OBAMA AND BLACK LIVES MATTER

by Derick Dailey

Over the course of the past eight years, America has witnessed an intensification of racial consciousness, consciousness that appears to have divided the country along racial lines, pitting the city against the suburbs, urban communities against rural ones, and people of color against non-people of color. Voting rights, community-police relations, housing, and education are all issues that have been at the fore of American political discourse since President Obama's election in 2008, and each issue significantly implicates race.

Race has played an important role in recent judicial opinions such as *Fisher* and *Shelby,* voter suppression efforts in states such as Texas and North Carolina, education debates related to public charter schools, and major protests in the aftermath of police-involved shootings and deaths in Ferguson, Baltimore, New York, and Florida, just to name a few. Race has been a predominant feature in the 2016 presidential election, reigniting our collective memory around terms and phrases such as "superpredator," the War on Drugs, mass incarceration, and welfare efforts of the 1990s. As the first African-American president of the United States, President Obama and his family implicate race for the country like no White House has ever done before, and in so doing, the Obama White House has called the country to greater racial awareness and subsequently greater collective dissonance.

What does this resurgence in race talk and race awareness do for an ever-browning America, and what lesson can we learn from President Obama's tactful and strategic handling of race as president? First, the resurgence of race talk is an indication that the country is engaged in collective racial consideration. That is to say that race is becoming un-ignorable, less taboo, and presents a unique opportunity for the country to engage in constructive racial dialogue. With an increase in African-American, Hispanic, and Asian constituencies, local, state, and national leaders are forced to speak more clearly to issues that affect communities of color and to work harder to address specific concerns of a more diverse electorate. As a consequence of the Obama White House, America is equipped with the necessary tools to begin the journey of racial reconciliation and racial justice. Consequently, post-Obama will be a *kairos* moment on the issue of race in America.

Second, President Obama's handling and mishandling of racial issues sends a clear signal to communities of color that raising racial consciousness is for all communities, not just white ones. President Obama spoke forcibly after the killings of Trayvon Martin and Michael Brown, made speeches to the NAACP and black churches, and established an important initiative aimed to support African-American males, but was slow, notwithstanding task forces and reports, to use his office to systematically address racial oppression. President Obama's resistance to go further is not purely political maneuvering; it also highlights a racial clash within the African-American community as it relates to ideological and policy positioning. Racial clash within the African-American community is not new. It was most pronounced during the Civil Rights movement with Rev. Dr. Martin Luther King, Jr. and Malcolm X. It was similarly apparent between Thurgood Marshall and Rev. Albert Cleage regarding the decentralization of public schools in Detroit, Michigan. Modern examples include Black Lives Matters ("BLM") and Rev. Jesse Jackson and Al Sharpton and the NAACP and African-American education activists regarding the public charter school movement.

President Obama's approach to race issues underscores the vi-brancy of racial clash within the African-American community on issues that deal with race. He, in many ways, attempted to balance the racial clash that currently exists, placing so-called more radical advocacy strategies against traditional strategies reminiscent of those employed during the Civil Rights move-ment. The African-American community has been challenged by President Obama to leverage its generational and ideological diversity in an attempt to work together to achieve racial justice. If the country takes advantage of this current moment of racial-ized discourse and considers the multitude of ways to address racial oppression, then President Obama's legacy will continue to inspire generations to come.

Derick Dailey is a Stein Scholar and third-year law student at Fordham University School of Law in New York. He is the National Chair of the National Black Law Students Association and a board member for Bread for the World and the Yale Black Alumni Association.

LEGISLATIVE AGENDA

Mr. President

NOT IN MY LIFETIME

by Rev. Dr. Gerald L. Durley

For a particular age group who grew up in America, it is not unrealistic to hear the familiar phrase, "Not in my lifetime." These words have been echoed by people of different races, cultures, and faiths when they reflect on the reality that an African-American had been elected president of the United States of America. Many believed, during their lifetime, that a Black person would never be elected to the presidency and certainly would not be elected for a second term. The very words "not in my lifetime" evoke the message that, due to unrealistic fears, widespread ignorance, and pervasive racism, the probability of an election of that magnitude could never have been won by an African-American. There were those who questioned whether a fair and equitable justice system for African-Americans would ever exist during their lifetime.

When Senator Barack H. Obama became president, the U.S. economy was in its worst recession since 1929. The unemployment rate was at an all-time high. The prison system was in dire need of reform. The nation had been dragged into questionable wars in the Middle East. Educational systems across the nation were not adequately educating all of their students. Racial sensitivity had resurfaced between Black and White Americans. There was distrust and disrespect at the highest levels among elected officials. Confidence in government leadership was virtually nonexistent.

Given the condition of the country that elected President Obama, I am thoroughly convinced that his enduring legacy will be extolled by the knowledge of his intense desire and determination to assure that America lived up to its constitutional mandate—in spite of all of the unfair, biased, hostile criticism that he faced, endured, and overcame for two terms. He believed in and governed on the basic principle set forth in the U.S. Declaration of Independence that we "…are created equal, … with certain unalienable Rights."

President Obama's record will reflect that he successfully negotiated a nuclear arms agreement with Iran; annihilated Osama bin Laden; re-established diplomatic relations with Cuba; and was sensitive to diverse groups that were relegated to the fringes of society. Believing that America was a melting pot for the world, President Obama was unafraid to challenge many of the basic civil, human, and economic rights that have been denied to many Americans. He was thrust into a "den of ruthless political lions" that pledged and vowed that he would be an unsuccessful, one-term president.

President Obama has had to lead while facing denials by a legislative body and an overly demanding American public. Black Americans wonder whether he could have done more to improve their standard and quality of life. Mexican-Americans continue to be gravely concerned about their citizenship status. The business and the health care industries feel that they were disrespected and unfairly treated under the Affordable Care Act of 2010, while numerous Americans express their intense concern about international terrorism.

A societal meltdown has emerged that seems to be dividing the nation ideologically, racially, economically, and politically. The historical account will record that President Obama courageously, conscientiously, and brilliantly stood in the gap to bridge the divide that has evolved.

I envision President Obama as a seasoned, nautical captain who has sailed the treacherous, unforgiving political storms of life where the waves of discouragement, discontentment, and doubt have attempted to deny his presidency from safely docking "Ship America" after an unimaginable eight-year voyage. The winds of adversity and opposition have been ever present, and his successful achievements have not always been clearly visible or understandable. However, he sailed on in spite of the foreboding negative political forecast. His resolute trust in God, confidence in his wife, love for his daughters, and his keen ability to keep the lines of communication open have allowed him to dock "Ship America" safely at several recognizably significant ports:

1) **Port Health Care:** A universal healthcare system now insures millions who thought they would not be insured "in my lifetime."

2) **Port Economic Recovery:** Here the unemployment rate has been reduced; the investment/banking industries have established financial accountability guidelines; more and new jobs were created; and the middle class believed that assistance would occur "in my lifetime."

3) **Port of Peace:** A port where American troops were brought home from around the world and diplomatic communications were established between America and other nations "in my lifetime."

4) **Port of Racial, Cultural, and Religious Diversity:** This port provides diverse populations the opportunity to openly discuss and seek viable solutions for living, working, and worshipping together. Docking at this port continues to be a challenge due to ignorance, fear, and greed.

5) **Port of Climate Change, Global Warming, and Environmental Justice:** This important and critical

port should be considered *the* civil and human rights issue facing the world today. President Obama steered "Ship America" toward policies that will protect humans, animals, plants, the air, and water for generations yet unborn. By signing international environmental treaties, President Obama is leaving office declaring that everyone has a God-endowed right to clean, unpolluted air; toxic-free water; affordable energy, and a healthier lifestyle.

President Obama will be remembered as an effective, sensitive, wise leader who was unafraid to dock "Ship America" in ports that other elected "captains" sailed past because of inevitable political turbulence. He has dared to make a significant difference for all Americans, and has established meaningful world relationships.

After his "captainship" as president, and as Barack H. Obama continues to sail and dock in future ports, let me reiterate that he has positively achieved that which I never believed possible— "not in my lifetime." I have survived long enough to know that when I hear or say, "Not in my lifetime," I can unreservedly and resoundingly affirm that an African-American was elected "in my lifetime," and America is far better because of President Barack H. Obama. Thank you, Mr. President!

Rev. Dr. Gerald L. Durley is Pastor Emeritus of the Providence Missionary Baptist Church of Atlanta, GA and a White House "Champion of Change" award recipient.

STRENGTHENING THE PRESENT AND FUTURE RELATIONSHIP BETWEEN THE USA AND AFRICA

by Rev. Dr. Angelique Walker-Smith

"The world will not be able to deal with climate change or terrorism, or expanding women's rights—all the issues that we face globally—without a rising and dynamic and self-reliant Africa. And that, more importantly than anything else, depends on a rising generation of new leaders. It depends on you."

President Barack Obama at the Town Hall with Mandela
Washington Fellows, August of 2016.

Growing up in Cedarville, Ohio was a difficult experience. Racism was blatant despite the presence of a major Christian college called Cedarville Bible College that my father attended at that time. Thanks to God's grace, our family's faith, togetherness, and our strong affirmation of African identity, we still prospered. Both our Christian and African identities were apparent in the books of our family's library and in our prayerful fellowship with the few other families of Africa and of African descent at the school. These experiences shaped my dream to go to Africa.

My dream came true after graduating from Yale University Divinity School. I became a Crossroader with Operation Crossroads Africa. My first of three assignments with Crossroads was in a village in the Darfur region of Sudan. These were all transformative experiences. Since that time I have travelled to 35 African countries and lived in six African countries. It was during these times that I deepened my understanding about the United States' public policy commitments to Africa. There were few attempts of mutual engagement with Africa that promoted

African self-reliance and growth as well as opportunities for young adults from the USA or Africa to engage in leadership development relative to Africa.

In 1958 Rev. Dr. James H. Robinson founded Operation Crossroads Africa, a nonprofit organization that still provides individuals with a seven-week experience in a nation in Africa. Founded on the principle that cultural immersion is possible through working and living inside Africa, their core values have been to challenge the assumptions individuals may have about Africa and to lead individuals to understand how African communities are formed and led by Africans. The legislation President J.F. Kennedy signed to create the Peace Corps was modeled after Operation Crossroads Africa. Operation Crossroads Africa also added the Crossroads African Leaders program that brought African leaders to the USA, in partnership with USAID and the VISTA program, as well as a Caribbean Crossroads program.

President Obama's legacy has furthered this agenda of young adult leadership development and mutual engagement with Africa. This has been done with a goal of African self-reliance and growth through the building of the economies and democracies of the nations of Africa in partnership with the heads of state in Africa and the African Union. President Obama has developed the Mandela Washington Fellowship, which is the flagship program of the president's Young African Leaders Initiative (YALI). This program, like Operation Crossroads, embodies President Obama's commitment to invest in the future of Africa. The program provides six weeks of intensive executive leadership training, networking, and skills building to accelerate career trajectories and contribute more robustly to strengthening democratic institutions, spurring economic growth, and enhancing peace and security in Africa.

President Obama's legacy has been outlined in the Obama Administration's U.S. Strategy Toward Sub-Saharan Africa that has led to the United States investing in development partnerships with Africans to foster sustained economic growth, promote food security, increase resilience to climate change, and improve the capacity of countries and communities to address HIV/AIDS, malaria, and other health threats. With President Obama's visible support came the bipartisan Congressional authorization of the African Growth Opportunities Act (AGOA) and its ten-year reauthorization. AGOA promotes free markets, expands U.S.-African trade and investment, stimulates economic growth, and facilitates sub-Saharan Africa's integration into the global economy. Through AGOA, the United States works with African countries to promote construction of infrastructure, improved business climate, regional economic integration, and trade preferences for exports to the United States. This legislation also furthers the USA's commitment to empower women through the African Women's Entrepreneurship Program (AWEP), an outreach, education, and engagement initiative. It targets African women entrepreneurs to promote business growth, increase trade both regionally and to U.S. markets through AGOA, create better business environments, and help African women entrepreneurs become agents of change in their communities.

Rev. Dr. Angelique Walker-Smith is Senior Associate for Pan African and Orthodox Church Relations.

Mr. President

PRESIDENT OBAMA AND THE POSSIBILITY OF ENDING HUNGER

by David Beckmann

President Barack Obama came to power in the midst of a huge financial crisis. It was also a hunger crisis. U.S. food insecurity surged by 30 percent as millions of Americans lost their jobs. One hundred million more people around the world were pushed into hunger because of the financial crisis coupled with a dramatic jump in grain prices.

The Obama stimulus package of 2009 helped keep the Great Recession from becoming a Depression. I remember my surprise and delight when Bread for the World analysts informed me that two-thirds of the stimulus spending was focused on low-income people. The expansion of SNAP, school lunches, tax credits, and other programs kept food security from rising further. Later, the Affordable Care Act extended health insurance to 13 million more people.

The elections of 2010 strengthened the caucus of extreme conservatives in Congress. They were uncompromising, and they managed to make their budget proposals the policy of the entire Republican Party in Congress. Starting in 2011, Republican budgets proposed deep cuts in government spending, with more than two-thirds of the cuts aimed at programs that serve low-income people. Their budgets from 2011 through 2016 each proposed to take away at least $3 trillion from low-income people over a period of ten years!

Bread for the World joined with other faith groups to insist on a "circle of protection" around programs focused on the needs of people in poverty. I was thrilled when the president met with us, and he was clearly touched by our closing prayer together. He defended low-income programs over years of tumultuous negotiations with Congress, and the cuts to federal anti-poverty programs were, in the end, minimal.

The U.S. economy gradually recovered, and in 2015 the extent of poverty and food insecurity in America finally started to drop as well. During President Obama's last year in the White House, I served on his Advisory Council on Poverty and Inequality. He took a series of administrative actions, notably on anti-racism reforms in the criminal justice system.

Bread for the World organizes people to lobby their members of Congress on changes to reduce hunger and poverty worldwide as well as in the United States. So I am keenly aware of President Obama's contributions to international development. Despite all the urgent issues confronting our own country as Obama came to office, he managed to address the economic crisis that had struck many of the world's poorest people. Even in his first inaugural address, he promised people in the poor nations of the world that the United States would "work alongside you to make your farms flourish" and "to nourish starved bodies and feed hungry minds."

At President Obama's first G8 Summit, he launched an international drive to help small-hold farmers in hungry countries increase their production and incomes. He doubled U.S. funding for agriculture and nutrition in Africa and other hard-hit parts of the developing world. By 2015, his Feed the Future program was investing in 9 million farm families and reaching 18 million children with nutrition assistance.

In recent decades, the world as a whole has been making unprecedented progress against hunger, poverty, and disease. The World Bank estimates that extreme poverty has been cut by more than half since 1990—from two billion people then to 776 million people in 2013. About half the countries in sub-Saharan Africa have made impressive economic gains and reduced poverty. In the United States, too, we have achieved some reduction in hunger and poverty over the decades. The economic crisis of 2008 was a major setback, but President Obama helped put our country and the world back on track toward the end of hunger and poverty.

The elections of 2016 were also a setback. Advocates need to do all in our power to defend the gains that were made in the Obama years and perhaps secure positive initiatives in a more adverse political environment.

In the fall of 2015, during Pope Francis's visit to our country, all the nations of the world agreed on the Sustainable Development Goals, which start with the goals of ending extreme poverty and hunger by 2030. President Obama spoke out strongly in favor of these goals and agreed that they apply to all countries, including the United States. He repeatedly told his advisors that he wants to be remembered as the U.S. president who put the world on track to end hunger and poverty.

That is how I will remember Barack Obama's presidency.

Reverend David Beckmann is President of Bread for the World.

Mr. President

ANONYMOUS CHARITY
by Rabbi Julie Schronfeld

When I look back at President Obama's eight years in office, I remember the heady feelings so many of us had on seeing our country's first African-American president elected with his inspiring First Lady Michelle; the optimism we had that our country finally had grown in important ways to take such a long-overdue step.

As events in our society have brought the persistent, deep structural racism into sharp focus and shattered some of that optimism, the historic importance of having this deeply thoughtful man as our president has only increased, and I appreciate his readiness to address complex issues and bring many voices to the table.

Of particular interest to me has been President Obama's willingness to address human trafficking, which includes sex trafficking, labor trafficking, forced child labor, and involuntary domestic servitude. Traffickers often exploit victims of war and economic inequality; they disproportionately prey on the poor, the homeless, and communities of color. President Obama's initiative in caring for the most vulnerable and neglected people on the planet, growing in numbers every day, is characteristic of the leader I know and admire.

Human trafficking is, as the president termed it, "one of the great human rights causes of our time." I was proud to serve on the President's Advisory Council on Faith-based and Neighborhood Partnerships that recommended the establishment of a department to deal specifically with human trafficking, and I was thrilled when the Office on Trafficking in Persons (OTIP) was created within the Department of Health and Human Services.

Thanks to this new office in our government, the United States can better support and help the thousands of individuals—men, women, and children of all backgrounds—who have been and continue to be trafficked within America's borders and to lead by example in aiding trafficked persons around the world.

Much work remains to be done in combating the evil of human trafficking, but just because the task is immense, it does not excuse us—or the world—from working diligently to make consistent progress. Our tradition teaches that saving one life is as if the entire world were saved. My organization, The Rabbinical Assembly, created its own effort to educate and amplify this work in all the communities around the world where we serve.

Jewish tradition teaches that the assistance we give anonymously to a person in need is the most highly praised, both because its motivation is to help another one of God's creatures and not to expand one's own reputation and also because such work is sensitive to the dignity of the person being helped. President Obama's landmark leadership in advancing the fight to stop human trafficking is not among his most publicized accomplishments, but it demonstrates the power of his thoughtful leadership that has always been concerned with the human condition and with the well-being of ordinary people the world over. In doing his part to work to end this great evil, he has shared in doing God's work.

Rabbi Julie Schonfeld is Executive Vice President of the Rabbinical Assembly (RA).

Mr. President

REFLECTION OF PRESIDENT BARACK H OBAMA

by Bishop Dr. Shirley Holloway

Mr. President, it is a known fact that prison reform can be perceived as a daunting and arduous undertaking when there is a determination to right some of those wrongs that continue to plague our society. The most powerful nation on earth, America is home to almost 5 percent of the world's population, yet it incarcerates approximately 25 percent of the imprisoned human population. Furthermore, our criminal justice system portrays a less than stellar performance when ranked with other world systems for impartiality, due process, rights of the accused, the effectiveness of criminal investigations, adjudications, and correctional systems, according to the 2015 *World Justice Project Rule of Law Index*. Also, our social service programs, rather than progressing toward the realization of the urgent need to provide more than adequate support for America's disenfranchised and marginalized citizens and communities, continue to maximize the use of jails and prison services as the answer to the country's moral dilemmas.

It is with these statistics in mind, along with the most recent historical data regarding the levels of discriminatory practices that exist within our criminal justice system, that I move to offer a vote of thanks for the work you have done thus far to repeal some of the most unfortunate and unfair prison sentences handed down to people of color.

Your journey, your story, brought hope to a people who otherwise would have found it difficult to believe that a black man could ever occupy the highest office in this nation, let alone be the leader of the free world. Once again, for this we thank you for working to close the disparity gap, but most importantly we thank God for "pre-destinating" your path in spite of the odds that were stacked against you. Hence, using your narrative regarding "the fierce urgency of now," we are hopeful for our young men that your planned work with the My Brother's Keeper initiative will forge a national alliance that is emboldened with the belief that all men are and were created equal; that within each individual lies the potential to be and become that which they were created to be; that we are more than the sum total of our experiences; and that it is through our own brokenness that we lean forward to care and cure ourselves and those whose lives we touch in such a way that change occurs and lives are restored. Mr. President, we are counting on you. Your legacy will chronicle the commitment made to be a catalyst of change for our citizens, for indeed lives of color do matter to God, to our nation, and to the world. Thank you, Sir.

Bishop Shirley Holloway, CEO of House Of Help City of Hope, Inc.

A CHANGED PEOPLE

by Bishop Kenneth W. Carter

As President Obama was assuming office in 2008, the Christian Methodist Episcopal Church began to encourage its members to learn how to navigate the challenging times by adopting a philosophy to move from good to great. It was the desire of the Episcopal leadership to encourage its hundreds of thousands of members to become an "Essential Church," poised for twenty-first century ministry. President Obama's "Faith-Based" initiative, which focused on the economy, education, energy and environment, and health care propelled the CME Church to make a cataclysmic shift and to focus our energies on investing in people and in our communities. We made sure our members had access to Obamacare and adequate health care insurance.

Our great nation made a tremendous stride in the election of the first African-American president of the United States of America. The election of Barack H. Obama marked many things, but perhaps the most important was that many, especially youth of various races, were freed from the mental slavery of not believing, not knowing that every man, woman, child is of equal importance and can aspire and achieve. The election of Barack Obama served as a catalyst, but it was his actual administration over the next eight years that would bring more inclusiveness and an atmosphere of inclusiveness, whether African American, Hispanic, White, Asian, Buddhist, Muslim, or Christian. While his election was a milestone, it has been his actual tenure and his years of service that modeled what it really means to be a citizen of the United States and to be unified in common goals and aspirations.

That's why our historic denomination, founded in 1870 by ex-slaves, shared the president's vision and urged its members to invest where we were and in each other. The church provided aid and outreach in Haiti, Africa, and elsewhere around the world while investing in our local communities. In doing so, we demonstrated our commitment to becoming a changed people devoted to changing the world.

The CME Church is proud to have stood with the Obama administration during these eight years and shall cherish and honor his tremendous legacy of leadership and service. All of the denominations who are a part of the faith community know that it was God's "Amazing Grace," so memorably sung by the president at the funeral in Charleston, that allowed him to lead us for such a time as this. We all thank God!

Kenneth W. Carter is presiding prelate of the Sixth Episcopal District of the Christian Methodist Episcopal Church.

THE UNFINISHED WORK OF HOPE AND CHANGE
by Dr. Earl B. Payton

"Yes We Can!" The crowds shouted as the nation, African-Americans in particular, bore witness to what American history told us was impossible, namely that a black man could ascend to the highest office in the land—president of the United States. In Grant Park, Barack Obama, with rhetorical splendor and with the cadence of the best of the black preaching tradition, became the symbol of hopes and dreams across generations.

Had the hope and change that I preached about over 30 years of ministry become a reality? Had the dream deferred by Langston Hughes become fulfilled before our eyes? Was it akin to what was said about Jesus: "Today this was fulfilled in your hearing"? Or was it more symbolic? In Barack Obama, the oppressed and the marginalized experienced the possibility of the nation living out its creed that all humans "are equal and endowed with certain inalienable rights." Hope and change. The crowd swayed and shouted, cried tears of joy with every word of his acceptance speech.

Personally, it is a night that will live with me forever. I will never forget how the youth marveled at the first African-American president with a measurable amount of adoration in their eyes. I recall that the elders blinked back tears because an impossible dream came true. For those who are old enough to remember Bloody Sunday and the riots in Detroit and Newark in the late 1960s, feelings of joy and pride were visible across their faces. Hanging on to every word, every thought and afterthought, in the eyes of many black men and women, I saw hope.

But as Obama approaches the culmination of his second and final term as President, there seems to be something missing. There seems to be unfinished work. African-Americans put an incredible amount of hope in Barack Obama, voting upwards of 90 percent for tangible change in dealing with the plight of Black America. Yet it appears at critical moments that the agenda of others overshadowed the agenda for jobs and justice. I'm aware that the institution of the presidency is greater than one individual. Still there was a missed opportunity to shape the national and international discourse on human rights and police brutality. To be honest, some days I/we feel betrayed.

On a weekly basis, the largest gatherings of African-Americans take place in Christian churches. When he was with us, the President Obama knew how to connect with us. One cannot minimize the influence his pastor, Dr. Jeremiah Wright, and the Trinity Church had in the formation of the young senator from Chicago. Barack Obama did his homework. In tragedy and in triumph, he walked with us, including at Charleston, South Carolina's Mother Bethel AME when he preached to our pain!

President Obama's campaigns were closely associated with black churches. He visited and spoke with us as we helped guide him to his victory. He would walk hand in hand with black preachers, prevailing through challenges and looking adversity in the eye, all to obtain the unconquerable. He heavily identified with our social issues and embodied our philosophies. But as the sensational energy associated with Obama's aura dwindled, so did the hope that begot the lost cause of the black agenda.

Though it was an accomplishment to have Barack Obama as the first African- American president, the sheer rhetoric of a black man being in office is not enough to alleviate pressures felt by the black community. We continued to witness many instances of systematic oppression and senseless murders. The birth of the Black Lives Matter movement consumed the media, but has yet to prompt a response from our first African-American president.

We thank God for President Obama and what he has done. The nation has not necessarily made change, but certainly in some respects it has made progress. As a leader, one is supposed to leave having put people in a better position to flourish than before one assumed the position. Unquestionably, in many respects the nation is on firmer ground than it was eight years ago.

Earl B. Payton is pastor of Sun City Christian Fellowship Baptist Church in El Paso, Texas and a retired U.S. Army chaplain.

MY BIGGEST DISAPPOINTMENT
by Dr. Felipe Martinez

It was late in the summer of 2008 and my preschool-age grandsons and I were volunteering for the Obama campaign. We went out canvassing in the Near Eastside of Indianapolis, visiting homes listed on the paperwork given to us by campaign organizers, encouraging people to turn out to the polls. I walked while my grandsons rode bikes, their helmets covered with Obama campaign stickers. For the most part, people were pleasant and open to conversation. Occasionally, however, we encountered rude push back from some people we contacted. There were racist comments that made me quite uncomfortable. Here I was, a Mexican immigrant with my two biracial grandchildren asking people to vote for Barack Obama, and I could sense that for some of my white neighbors the prospect of having our first African-American president brought racist feelings to the surface. The tension felt so personal, so intense.

That election was personal for me, too. It was the first presidential election in which I could vote as a brand new United States citizen. It was exciting to see my adoptive state of Indiana go blue in a presidential election. It was inspiring to see people coming together under the ideas and hopeful vision President Obama was setting forth. As his first term unfolded, I, along with other Latinos, waited patiently as important agenda items were addressed (economic recovery, universal health care), and we knew that eventually there would come the time for comprehensive immigration reform, an item so important to us. Justice in immigration is more than a personal issue for me: it is a theological issue. The scriptures offer clear guidance for protection of the foreigners in our midst, reminding us of God's care for the people on the margins and connecting us to our historical immigrant roots. It is also a moral issue. We as a country benefit greatly from the hard work of our immigrants (documented and undocumented alike). We value their work, but we don't value the workers, leaving them vulnerable as we force so many to an underground economy.

Unfortunately, we never got comprehensive immigration reform. I understand that the political environment changed, and that in spite of bipartisan efforts to make it come about, obstructionist congressional leaders succeeded in sinking it. Millions of immigrants had hoped they could come out of the shadows. Millions of Dreamers were kept from their American Dream. Even when President Obama attempted to cut through the obstruction with an Executive Order to offer some hope, the process stalled in the courts.

President Obama and his administration moved the needle on the subject of immigration reform, just not far enough. It remains my single biggest disappointment about his presidency, though I suspect it is not nearly as disappointing to me as it is to him.

I am grateful for President Obama's leadership these past eight years. I pray that the vision he offered for immigration reform will become a reality in the near future.

Rev. Dr. Felipe N. Martinez is Pastor of First Presbyterian Church in Columbus, IN.

THE POSITIVE INFLUENCE OF STRONG WOMEN
by Dr. Willie Gable

One cannot reflect on the man President Barack H. Obama and not acknowledge that he is the humble processor of a myriad of firsts, which are surely too numerous to mention in this brief reflection. There is no debate that the unseen hand of Divinity has not only "ordered his steps," but has orchestrated his successes. It is quite apparent that this sanctified pilgrimage has a heavenly purpose yet to be revealed. However, within the woven tapestry of his life are sacred angels that have shaped and influenced him.

President Obama has had and still has strong women who trigger his imagination and challenge his perspectives on the life he must live. As a young lad growing up, he mastered the art of living in a virtual interactive world where he constantly had to ask that penetrating question, "Who am I?" The strong women helped navigate him through this mist we call life. The Affordable Health Care Act may be his signature legislation; however, it is not coincidental that his first action as president was the signing of the Lilly Ledbetter Fair Pay Act.

First his mother, Ann Dunham, in whom he saw virtue and a never-give-up spirit, formed his foundation to meet adversity without being adverse. His mother's voyages into uncharted waters at that time in America's history were cataclysmic. As an analytic-autonomizer, Mr. Obama keeps seeking more information that forms the basis for decisions. His mother nurtured that quality in him.

Then there was Madelyn Dunham, his grandmother. During his teen years, this strong woman shaped his phase of thinking as he pushed himself onto the margins of life. Grandmother's steady hand of wisdom provided a compass that would direct him for years. And in 1989 Michelle Robinson would become the anchor that allowed him to seek heights unknown for most black men. First, Michelle Obama would challenge his theology, philosophy, and sociology. For the man who kept the virtual interactive wall around himself, he now was grounded with a full partner who would always have an encouraging word during times of darkness. There indeed were other strong women in his life—Marian Robinson and, of course, Malia and Sasha and many more whose thoughts, words, and lives encourage him to move even when the way is blocked.

President Obama's legacy is set and never to be changed as the first African-American president, one who, because of strong women who nurtured and molded him, would be always thinking with his heart and five moves ahead of his opponents. Much will be written and said about President Obama in the future, some true and some unfortunately untrue. But the divine steps that were ordered have also guided the ordained struggles. This is not to say he did not make some mistakes in his eight-year tenure, but it is to say that when he did, there was the unseen hand righting the wrong and making the crooked places straight.

Rev. Dr. Willie Gable, Jr., D.Min., is Pastor of Progressive Baptist Church in New Orleans, LA and Chairman of the National Baptist Convention USA, Inc. Housing and Economic Development Board.

PRESIDENT OBAMA: CHAMPION FOR LOW-WAGE WORKERS AND WORKING FAMILIES
by Phil Tom

President Obama was a champion for protecting workers' rights and strengthening policies to support working families. In working with Secretary of Labor Hilda L. Solis and Thomas E. Perez, the U.S. Department of Labor developed new regulations and administrative interpretations to support low-wage workers and working families. On October 1, 2013, the U.S. Department of Labor revised its regulations defining companionship services so that many direct care workers, such as certified nursing assistants, home health aides, personal care aides, and other caregivers, would be protected by the Federal Labor Standards Act. When the Fair Labor Standards Act (FLSA) was enacted in 1938 to provide minimum wage and overtime protections for workers, it excluded workers employed directly by households in domestic service. This rule primarily impacted low-wage women workers of color.

The Department of Labor (DOL) <u>estimates</u> that there are two million workers providing home care to children, the elderly, or the disabled, including those employed by third-party agencies. The U.S. Department of Labor's Wage and Hour Division issued several administrators' interpretations that strengthen its ability to combat wage theft, misclassification, and joint employment practices by employers impacting low-wage and middle-income workers such as fast food workers and store managers. On April 6, 2016, the U.S. Department of Labor finalized a rule that would address conflicts of interests on retirement advice, saving middle class families billions of dollars every year. The Department's conflict of interest final rule will protect investors by requiring all who provide retirement investment advice to plans, plan fiduciaries, and IRAs to abide by a "fiduciary" standard—putting their clients' best interests before their own profits. This rule fulfilled the Department's mission to protect, educate, and empower retirement investors as they face important choices in saving for retirement in their IRAs and employee benefit plans. On May 18, 2016, President Obama and Secretary Perez announced the publication of the Department of Labor's final rule updating the overtime regulations, which extended overtime pay protections to over 4 million workers. This long-awaited updated rule realized President Obama's commitment to ensuring every worker is compensated fairly for their hard work.

However, because of the resistance of a Republican-controlled Congress to enact legislation to raise the minimum wage and to provide paid leave to support low-wage workers and working families, President Obama issued several executive orders to support workers employed by federal contractors. On February 12, 2014, President Obama signed Executive Order 13658, "Establishing a Minimum Wage for Contractors," to raise the minimum wage to $10.10 for all workers on federal construction and service contracts. On September 7, 2015, President Barack Obama signed Executive Order (EO) 13706, Establishing Paid Sick Leave for Federal Contractors. The Executive Order requires certain parties that contract with the Federal Government to provide their employees with up to 7 days of paid sick leave annually, including paid leave allowing for family care.

During his eight years, President Obama and his U.S. Department of Labor made great strides in improving the lives for millions of American workers and their families.

Rev. Phil Tom served in President Obama's administration as Director of the Center for Faith-based and Neighborhood Partnerships for the U.S. Department of Labor, 2010-2015.

Mr. President

THE NEW ABOLITIONISM: OBAMA MONETARY REFORM AND THE FUTURE OF CIVIL RIGHTS

by Delman Coates, Ph.D.

As the sun prepares to set on the historic presidency of President Barack Obama, I am reminded of that day (November 4, 2008) when the newly elected president, Michelle Obama, Sasha, and Malia walked out and addressed the crowd at Grant Park in Chicago to give his victory speech. We were filled with so much optimism and hope. Television images showed celebrities, civil rights leaders, and average Americans literally in tears, having witnessed what most people never thought was possible in their lifetime: an African American elected president of the United States of America. There was so much emotion because of the sense that President Obama's ascension was finally the fulfillment of all our hopes and dreams. This is what our ancestors fought for, and the belief was that this marked a significant turning point in America that would ensure peace and prosperity for our children and our children's children.

This conviction was so palpable that political pundits and cultural commentators were calling Obama's election the end of an era characterized by race in America. The *LA Times* did a piece titled, "Obama's Post-racial Promise." *Forbes* magazine went so far as to declare, "Racism in America Is Over." And *US News & World Report* published a piece titled, "President-Elect Barack Obama: A Post-racial President Who Should Focus the Country on Race."

Eight years after so much optimism, the national mood has shifted, as race is once again center stage in America with the senseless police shootings of unarmed black men and women, the Mother Emmanuel AME Church tragedy in 2015 in Charleston, SC, and the emergence of the Black Lives Matter movement. Rather than the last eight years being marked by the best in America, we have seen the worst. Challenges to the Voting Rights Act; the Flint, Michigan water crisis; and a presidential campaign in which the victor stoked the flames of racism, Islamophobia, and xenophobia have reminded us that overcoming the legacy of American racism will require more than the ascension of one individual from the historically oppressed masses to the highest office in the land.

After having to console my children in the wake of this year's election result, I am convinced that the path forward requires a more thorough understanding of the way in which economic issues structure, determine, and intersect with matters of race. Any vision of American progress that ignores economic realities will be ineffective at solving the issues facing the country. There can be no mistaking the fact that one of the crowning achievements of the Obama presidency has been the economic recovery from the worst recession since the Great Depression. President Obama inherited an 8% unemployment rate and an average monthly job loss of 700,000. Under the Obama administration, more than 10 million jobs have been added, job openings are at a 15-year high, and the buying power of the average weekly worker's paycheck increased 4.4% (as of July 2016). As of 2015, the jobless rate for African Americans was reduced 50%, from 16.7% to 8.3%.

These benefits, however, have come at a huge cost for the country. The national debt during President Obama's tenure has increased from $8 trillion to almost $20 trillion. This unsustainable level of national debt is the result of funding economic stimulus through government borrowing from private banks. The resulting interest on the national debt places a burden of taxation on the American people, adversely impacts the quality of life for all Americans, fuels wealth concentration, and deprives the nation of the resources it needs to expand American prosperity to the most vulnerable Americans. At the current rate of borrowing, it is projected that by the time current kindergarten children enter college in 2030, our national debt with be 116% of GDP and by 2040, 151%.

While borrowing as a means of creating economic stimulus leads to short-term benefits, the long-term disadvantages ought to force us to imagine an alternative means of stimulating the economy, creating jobs, and investing in underserved communities, something that does not rely on private, bank-issued, debt-based money. Most Americans, including politicians, have no real understanding of our monetary system and do not understand the way in which our debt-based monetary system creates inequality, destabilizes our society, and produces discourses of difference based on such factors as class, race, and gender

What do I mean by this? Well, in order for the government, businesses, and citizens to obtain money for infrastructure, schools, job creation, mortgages, social programs, education, and more, we have to borrow money from private banks, money that has to be paid back with interest. When banks place money into circulation for these purposes, they issue the principal amount of money, but not the interest. This mechanism of our economic system creates economic scarcity and forces the public into competition for non-existent resources.

A simple example here is in order. Imagine a mythical society of 10 people who are each issued $1,000 that has to be returned at 10% interest. The problem is that $10,000 is in circulation ($1,000 X 10), but the 10 people owe the banker $11,000. There is no amount of legislation, education, taxation, hard work, or prayer to account for this mathematical problem or what some have called "money scarcity." Such a society can only be sustained by the infusion of more borrowing, or "stimulus" to stimulate economic activity, which has the residual effect of further enslaving the society with more debt. This is the reason the very financial institutions that created the global financial crisis (for which they have not been held accountable) are now three times larger than they were before the Great Recession.

While our society is much larger and much more robust than this simplified example, the same principle applies. In a debt-based monetary system, there's not enough money in circulation to meet the needs of the people in the society. Therefore, in a debt-based monetary system discourses of difference (e.g., race, gender, xenophobia) become unjust strategies to determine the allocation of scarce economic resources.

If we want a just society, we must have a just money system, one that fixes the underlying conditions of our monetary system that cause members of our society to be in competition for non-existence resources. It does not have to be this way. Rather than funding national priorities (e.g., jobs, public education, health care, defense, infrastructure, environmental protections, and more) through private, bank-issued, debt-based money, America can and should fund its priorities through government-issued, interest-free money. This would help all Americans by reducing inflation, reducing the tax burden, reducing wealth concentration, and providing the necessary resources to invest in America. Rather than enriching the financial elite through the paying of interest on debt-based money, government issued interest-free money would enable our society to invest in the American people whose labor produces America's wealth. By eliminating the economic scarcity that is baked into any debt-based money system, we reduce the need for discourses of difference being the prevailing prism through which people in a free society have to interact with one another.

Government-issued, interest-free money would enable the country to reap the economic benefits of Obama's tenure in office without being shackled by the economic burdens of debt-based money. By funding the national recovery through borrowing debt-based money, the ultimate beneficiaries of the nation's recovery are the private banks that issue the nation's debt-based money. An approach to monetary policy that empowers the government to issue its own money, interest-free to itself, enables the nation's prosperity to flow to the American people whose hard work and labor produce America's wealth rather than flowing to the unproductive labor of the financial elite who merely issue the nation's debt-based money.

We are at a critical point in American public life, and we have an opportunity to advance an alternative theory of social change and economic justice, one that breaks the burden of taxation due to borrowing from private banking interests and that grounds American public policy in government-issued, interest-free money to promote the public good. The next human and civil rights frontier involves a thorough understanding of our monetary system and a reclamation of a theology of economics central in scripture and in the history of the Christian church. According to scripture, "the borrower is slave to the lender." As such, we are in need of an economic abolitionist movement that frees American public policy from the bondage of debt-based money and provides a unifying metanarrative for those concerned about justice, equality, peace, and prosperity in this land.

Rev. Delman Coates, Ph.D., is Senior Pastor at Mt. Ennon Baptist Church (Clinton, MD).

THE GOSPEL OF OBAMACARE

by Dr. Kip Banks

I was blessed to attend a Faith Leader Policy Roundtable in the last months of President Barack Obama's administration, and I thank God that over the eight years of his presidency I was able to attend similar meetings. It is truly a blessing that during the Obama administration, African American clergy persons like me have had input into White House policymaking. Needless to say, I will miss President Barack Obama and all those who worked so capably within his administration. Overall, I think President Obama has done an excellent job, especially given that he's faced so much outright opposition from the U.S. Congress and a climate of economic and racial hostility. Indeed, President Obama's very existence as an African American man occupying the highest office in the land for two terms is a message to us all that with God all things are possible! (Matthew 19:26).

However, President Obama wasn't content just to occupy the office; he also sought to use his God-given talents and abilities to champion the causes of the most vulnerable in our society, consistent with the 25th chapter of the Gospel of Matthew, which instructs us to care for the "least" of our brothers and sisters. The bottom line is that President Obama cared, and this was reflected in the many pieces of legislation that he signed into law on behalf of the least in our society.

The changes on behalf of the poor and vulnerable were profound. What Obama did was change the way we produce and consume energy, the way doctors and hospitals treat us, the academic standards in our schools, and the long-term fiscal trajectory of the nation. Also, gays can now serve openly in the military, insurers can no longer deny coverage because of preexisting conditions, credit card companies can no longer impose hidden fees, and markets no longer believe the biggest banks are too big to fail. Solar energy installations are up nearly 2,000 percent, and carbon emissions have dropped even though the economy is growing.

Among the president's greatest achievements was the passage of the Affordable Care Act (ACA), also known as Obamacare. Although some have taken to malign Obamacare, for many it has been good news. In fact, at the last White House briefing that I attended, a bishop testified that prior to Obamacare his family was almost in financial ruin because they couldn't afford to pay for prescription medications, but once Obamacare was passed their medication became affordable.

Of course, the law is not perfect, but the bottom line is that 20 million people who didn't have health insurance now have it, and this is good news! Furthermore, although health care costs and premiums will rise, they will rise much more slowly than they did during the George W. Bush administration and over the past 50 years.

However, it's up to us to protect Obamacare and the many other pieces of legislation that President Obama signed into law. In fact, I believe that in the wake of the Obama administration, God is calling us as people of faith to advocate at the federal, state, and local levels for policies that will take care of the least of our brothers and sisters. This includes expansion of Obamacare and legislation to combat climate change and to reform our nation's prison industrial complex.

President Obama campaigned on the theme "Yes We Can," and now it's up to us to believe that we can continue his legacy of care and compassion for the least of our brothers and sisters. Ultimately, we must understand that Obama's presidency was a direct product of the legacy of the African American church, and as a church we must continue to fight in faith for justice for all until that day when justice rolls down like waters and righteousness like a mighty stream.

Dr. Kip Banks is the senior pastor of East Washington Heights Baptist Church in Washington, DC.

MY BROTHER'S KEEPER
by Dr. Eddie Connor

Dr. Martin Luther King declared, "We must learn to live together as brothers or perish together as fools."

As a native of Detroit, Michigan, I know that brotherhood and togetherness are not often the ties that bind our communities. Many of the urban communities in America are tirelessly in pursuit of adequate housing and education, safe communities, upward mobility, and longevity of life.

Barack Hussein Obama embodies the struggle and strength of our ancestors—from the transatlantic slave trade, to *Brown v. Board of Education*, to the March on Washington, to the steps of the National Mall as he was sworn in as the 44th president of the United States of America.

President Barack Obama's rise to ascension unfolded under the rage of racism in America. We witnessed the national traumas of Trayvon Martin, Michael Brown, Tamir Rice, Freddie Gray, Walter Scott, and many other black boys and men who were victims of vitriolic racial violence.

A biracial president who was bipartisan affirmed, "I've got relatives who look like Bernie Mac and I've got relatives who look like Margaret Thatcher." He bridged the racial divide of identity in his family and sought to heal the wounds of a country that he loves dearly. President Obama became a symbol of hope for unity when the United States was divided.

The great abolitionist Frederick Douglass declared, "If we build strong children we won't have to repair broken adults." I like to say, "If we build strong boys, we won't have to repair broken men."

In his My Brother's Keeper initiative, President Obama spoke to a racially charged criminal justice system, the onslaught of police brutality, and a skewed education system of low literacy levels. He confronted the issue that black and brown youth are expelled from school at higher rates than whites, exacerbating the "Preschool-to-Prison Pipeline."

President Obama's My Brother's Keeper initiative tackles persistent opportunity gaps faced by boys and young men of color. The initiative develops a sustainable structure of six milestones to ensure that our boys and young men reach their fullest potential. President Obama issued a clarion call for our communities to galvanize the greatness within our children. I, along with millions of other black men across America, are transforming lives by mentoring and developing young giants for greatness.

President Obama expressly shows America what it often fails to accept. Despite the negative media portrayals and stereotypes, black men are strong fathers, leaders, scholars, mentors, entrepreneurs, teachers, and advocates for their communities.

The opportunity to give black and brown brothers a seat at the table changes their trajectory for success. President Obama understands that if we are not at the table we will be on the menu. A seat at the table of brotherhood is what will provide breakthrough.

Growing up without a father in my life, I was constantly in search of my identity. At the age of fifteen, I was dealt a death blow, being diagnosed with stage four cancer. In high school, my guidance counselor told me that I would never go to college. Yet through diligence and perseverance, I not only graduated but today I am a college professor. Through faith in God and the prayers of a loving mother, I am not only surviving but thriving today and working to make a difference.

A black man in the White House brought style and swagger, like James Brown's poetry in motion: "Say it loud, I'm black and I'm proud." His substance and sophistication bellows from his words, "Change will not come if we wait for some other person or some other time. We are the ones we've been waiting for. We are the change that we seek."

As a millennial, I salute President Obama's service to our nation, his dedication, and his willingness to embrace those who rejected him. His efforts serve as a constant reminder that "life's most persistent and urgent question is, 'What are you doing for others?'". Our children can grow up in a world today where being a black president is no longer an anomaly; it's a reality. On behalf of youth and millennials in America, thank you, President Obama, for your dedication and service to our nation. Through difficulty and doubt, you inspired us to believe that "Yes, We Can" transform our community, our country, and our world.

Dr. Eddie Connor is bestselling author, international speaker, and CEO of the literacy organization Boys 2 Books.

Mr. Barack Hussein Obama:
A 5-Star President

by Dr. Amos Brown

"If a man does not keep pace with his companions, perhaps it is because he hears a different drummer. Let him step to the music which he hears, however measured or far away."

-Henry David Thoreau in *Walden*

Without fear of contradiction I submit that Mr. Barack Hussein Obama is a man of character and integrity. He is a humble intellectual who has brought class and precision to the White House, not just an excellent statesman and an admired husband and father. Many Americans will undoubtedly be emotional when President Barack Obama departs the Oval Office. I will be among them. We will miss his genuine smile and quick wit, but more than anything we will bid farewell to one of the most accomplished presidents in history.

President Obama's resume offers bullet points from a deliberative man who not only understands issues, but plans for them. The Harvard-educated attorney brought a respect for training and competency to the White House, but he rejected elitism and arrogance. He tackled every issue with a calm sense of respect for other points of view, without caving in when what is right was on the line. Despite backlash from the healthcare industry, for example, he successfully pushed for the Affordable Healthcare Act, otherwise known as Obamacare. It became the first true, sweeping reform of how the nation prevents illness and treats its sick in the spirit and manner of Jesus of Nazareth. Now, millions more Americans are insured while the overall long-term cost of healthcare is being reduced.

Mr. President showed the same deliberativeness, compassion, and common sense when establishing the My Brother's Keeper Challenge, a public-private partnership promoting intervention by civic and faith leaders into the lives of young men of color, which also promotes racial justice. He wanted black lives to know they matter, not just by saying it but by doing something about racial justice. His compassion was also mixed with courage when he pushed for the Marriage Equality Act, providing equal protection under the law to gay couples. To use the words of Sweet Daddy Grace, he knows how to "tangabilitate" the gospel of love.

Moreover, Mr. Obama pushed for what's right in the face of vigorous and at times nasty pushback from a powerful conservative force that may have slowed, but failed to halt, his policies based on justice and compassion. While conservatives may not like the president's policies or points of view, it is difficult for anyone to degrade Mr. Obama as a person and family man who has not brought disgrace to the White House. His integrity, mixed with his calm temperament, has been integral to the president's many accomplishments. His ability to control his anger and to maintain poise and decorum is a rare and crucial quality to being a successful commander-in-chief. He was able to enact social justice without alienating groups of Americans. His mantra was "no one left behind."

President Obama and Secretary of State Clinton shared a calmness and coolness under fire when making the crucial calls to capture Osama Bin Laden. After the successful raid, Obama and his staff showed a confidence and poise that made Americans—both Democrats and Republicans—feel not only victorious, but safe.

Mr. Obama backed all Americans even though some (including his own half-brother) declined to back him. Being racially mixed, he weathered with courage accusations that he wasn't black enough or that he was not an American or Christian. Rather than respond, Mr. Obama led the charge to ensure that immigrants who have been living and contributing to our nation for decades have a real opportunity to achieve citizenship. What we have seen in Mr. Obama as a politician is what we see in him as a family man. But when he is up on that podium addressing the world, we witness a maestro who has the chemistry to read his audience. As an orator, he achieved quintessential cadences and displayed an extreme talent for connecting with an audience, from small groups to large stadiums and even across a television screen. He brought both substance and style to speech. It is a chemistry cloaked by the principle that the United States must be governed for the people and by the people. With all the aforementioned accomplishments and more, he has certainly proven to be a 5-Star president and a man of the people.

Mr. President, when I think of you I think of the words of the poet Edwin Markham from the poem "Outwitted": "They drew a line that shut me out, Heretic, rebel, a thing to flout! But love and I had the wit to win. We drew a circle and brought them in."

Rev. Dr. Amos C. Brown is Senior Pastor at the Third Baptist Church of San Francisco and Chairman of the Social Justice Commission of the National Baptist Convention, USA.

ON MAKING AMERICA BETTER

by Dr. Marthenia "Tina" Dingle Dupree

It was a historic day: the U.S. presidential election in 2008 when a senator, a community organizer, a young black man whose mother was white and his father black from the Motherland of Kenya, Africa was elected to become the most powerful man in the world. Barack H. Obama, the 44th president of the United States of America, was inaugurated on January 20, 2009, one of the most historic moments in our country since the beginning of our nation.

This election dominated the media worldwide. There was no story bigger than this one. Never in our history! The New York Times headline was, "Obama Wins Election." Messages from heads of state came from around the world: Algeria, Egypt, Argentina, the Bahamas, Brazil, Canada, Colombia, Jamaica, Afghanistan, China, India, Japan, France, Greece, Ireland, Russia, the United Kingdom, Israel, and many more. The BBC News/Africa/Kenya headline read, "Kenya declares holiday for Obama." The president of Kenya, Mwai Kibaki, announced a public holiday in honor of Obama's victory. The BBC included a quote in an article by Nelson Mandela, South Africa's first black president, who wrote in a letter of congratulations, "Your victory has demonstrated that no person anywhere in the world should not dare to dream of wanting to change the world for a better place."

Millions of people were filled with great joy and excitement for this history-making event. Others, such as Rev. Jesse Jackson, who for years endured the struggle for black people, had tears streaming down, possibly reflecting on the time in our history when this would not have been possible. The first elected African-American president of the United States of America! This writer also cried tears of joy, but with a little concern that the celebrated "first" would meet with many challenges to be an effective commander-in-chief. The world would constantly be watching. And this writer would constantly be praying.

Just a short time after the celebrations, America gave the president a huge challenge. There was one financial disaster after another. In my heart, I was thinking that this was a plan of the Republicans. After all, I do believe that they control a huge amount of the wealth in America and a large number of elected officials. Perhaps I am just a dreamer, but I have always believed that they were planning their platform against this president from the start. This is just my point of view. Some of the students at the university where I was teaching at the time called this control group "The Illuminati." Today's youth are smarter than we believe them to be.

Okay, I apologize for the brief rant. Now back to some of the significant challenges that our president began to face as newly-elected commander-in-chief. It started with the housing bubble, then sub-prime loans, then huge bank failures, then the stock market crashing, bringing the economy into a recession and high unemployment. So now starts the blamers. I believe this was also a part of their platform—to wait for an opportunity to start a campaign that would bring doubt into the minds of the American people about the president's ability to effectively handle critical situations. The previous administration had begun to implement the bailout of the banks and had already set a date and time to return our troops home from the wars in Iraq and Afghanistan. The media began to play the blame game with not much mention that these effects on the economy were already implemented by the previous administration.

However, during this first term--sweet victory. In 2010 major health care reform was passed. YEAH! Millions of Americans were able to get affordable health care despite pre-existing conditions. Some for the first time received health care. The challengers began to surface, using this new health care bill as their footstool. They began to poke and make fun of the bill by calling it OBAMACARE. Our president, never losing his cool or his swagger, stated that he liked the name and it became the brand of the people for health. A survey shows that millions of Americans like OBAMACARE but not the Affordable Health Care Act, even though they are the same.

In my point of view, President Barack H. Obama has made America better. Since 1900 only six Democratic U.S. presidents have been re-elected. In his State of the Union address in 2012, the president said it best: "I have no more campaigns to run," and as his opponents applauded, he fired back: "I know, because I won both of them."

Dr. Marthenia "Tina" Dingle Dupree is a community leader, author, radio host, and President & Founder of Professional Speakers Network, Inc.

A PRESIDENT FOR ALL PEOPLE
by Jo Anne Lyon

Watching the Democratic Convention of 2004, I thought, "Everyone sounds alike; is there no fresh vision?" Just as I was flipping to another channel, Senator Barack Obama took the stage. From the moment he began speaking, I was captivated. The personal story, the urgency in his voice, the intellectual capacity, and the thoughtfulness compelled me. From that moment on, I began to follow his journey from afar.

I, along with millions of people, had tears in my eyes as I listened to his acceptance speech in Grant Park. The power of the moment reminded me of the hundreds of thousands who have fought the fight of racial injustice for over a hundred years. Yes, there is Hope, and change is evident.

As a faith leader, I know that the issue of immigration reform has impacted our churches and communities for years. Therefore, when President Obama continued these conversations I was encouraged. As a result, I had the privilege to meet with him on two separate occasions regarding the issue. On one occasion, it was in the Roosevelt Room with other members of the National Association of Evangelicals. As he walked into the room, there was a presence of humility and care for each of us. We openly discussed the issue, and he shared how his faith informed these decisions of caring for the stranger.

On another occasion I was privileged to meet with him in the Oval Office. Here there were only six of us to discuss more fully the stories that are happening on the ground with undocumented people and, in particular, our church leaders. He listened intently as I described the mistreatment of one of our pastors as an example of our broken system. We discussed the need for prayer in these issues as well. As we were ready to leave, he requested that we pray, then suggested that we stand and join hands. He asked one of our colleagues to pray. It was a very humbling moment as we stood in the most revered room of the world with the president of the most powerful country on the planet who was humbly calling on God for greater wisdom.

President Obama did not only care and talk about the issue of immigration, but also used his executive powers for the people. I have found him to be a person who after much thought will take risks for what he believes is right and for the good of the people.

It has been my honor to serve on the President's Council on Faith and Neighborhood Partnerships. Our particular priority has been that of poverty and inequity. At our first meeting, as I listened to his various domestic policy advisers speak about things such as the programs in place, what was in the future, and how to evaluate and make it better, I was struck by the intensity of their commitment to the mission and vision. There was absolutely no slacking off. They were in this for the long haul. This instilling in his staff reflected the tireless vision of President Obama.

Issues of mass incarceration and policing have been ones most leaders have avoided. Again, President Obama was willing to take risks for the good of the people. His continued release of nonviolent offenders from the long sentences they have been assigned has given thousands new hope and a second chance. The money provided for college education within many prisons is equipping people to achieve a dream they never thought was possible, enabling them to make new choices that benefit them and society. In addition, naming and attempting to solve the issues of policing exhibits strength of character and the desire to govern for all.

President Obama also sees the world's global interconnectedness. There are many examples of this, but one in which I was involved is that of Ebola. When the crisis hit, people in the US thought it would not impact them. After all, these are just poor countries in West Africa that no one knows about. Almost, "let the people die." President Obama immediately began to call people to the White House for discussion. I had the privilege to be one of those people to come to discuss what our faith community was doing and how we could all work together. However, the American people soon saw how one person with Ebola from a failed state (Liberia) coming to Dallas with Ebola melted down their health system. Yes, as the president knew so well – we are interconnected in a very complex world. President Obama has been a president for all people, both in the United States and the world.

Dr. Jo Anne Lyon is the Vice President of Wesley Seminary in Marion, Indiana.

HOLDING US ACCOUNTABLE: DACA AS PROCLAMATION OF HOPE & CHANGE

by Rev. Richard A. Burnett

"On January 1, 1863, Abraham Lincoln presided over the annual White House New Year's reception. Late that afternoon, he retired to his study to sign the Emancipation Proclamation. When he took up his pen, his hand was shaking from exhaustion. Briefly, he paused – 'I do not want it to appear as if I hesitated,' he remarked. Then Lincoln affixed a firm signature to the document."

(Eric Foner, The New York Times Op-Ed,
Tuesday January 1, 2013)

More than a few parallels have been drawn between President Lincoln and President Obama since a young state senator from Illinois set ablaze moral imaginations and renewed hope in a speech nominating the 2004 Democratic presidential candidate. The shared home state, the short service in the U. S. Senate, the pragmatic folk wisdom and transcendental rhetoric on gun violence, race in American life, and respect for those we would name our "enemy" make remarkable links between the two men. However, nothing comes as close for me as the connections between Lincoln's executive order of 1863 to emancipate all persons held in slavery in the United States and the executive action of 2012 (expanded in 2014) known simply as DACA.

This landmark executive action—Deferred Action for Childhood Arrivals ("DACA")—was in part a response by President Obama to the disappointment he and many other Americans felt when legislation recognizing and supporting undocumented immigrant children and students known as "Dreamers" failed in the U.S. Congress. During the days leading up to The Dream Act presentation on Capitol Hill, I spoke from the pulpit and at the Ohio state house in strong support of the reforms that would put into law the same spirit expressed in biblical injunctions to remember the stranger: "The alien who resides with you shall be to you as the citizen among you; you shall love the alien as yourself; for you were aliens (also)." (Leviticus 19:34). We at Trinity Church pledged our support, our prayers, our dollars, and our passion to those Dreamers who piled into buses coming from the West Coast and across country, through Columbus, toward our nation's capital to cry freedom for young people who, as one brave student named Maria said at Trinity days before Easter Sunday: "I will not live in the shadows any longer…I am undocumented and I am a dreamer!" That day I saw resurrection happen.

DACA is Barack Obama's "Amen" to Maria and thousands like her. According to the Pew Research Center, up to 1.7 million people could have been eligible for the DACA status put forward in 2012. States and federal courts are having mixed responses to this executive action, and this comes as no surprise given today's polarizing tenor. But I am convinced that DACA—rising boldly from the grave of The Dream Act—will be greeted by history with approval and thanks.

Mr. President

A Columbus community organizer who led me to support the Dreamers before they rode the buses to Washington tells me of an encounter he experienced with President Obama following his first inauguration. "Hold me accountable," he told the advocates when pressed for Comprehensive Immigration Reform. Thus, the Dreamers did hold Barack Obama accountable. And by his executive action, DACA, the president holds us all accountable, because, like Lincoln, Obama "affixed a firm signature" for a lasting hope.

Rev. Richard A. Burnett is Rector at Trinity Episcopal Church, Capitol Square, in Columbus, OH.

THE OBAMA LEGACY

Mr. President

A TEMPLATE FOR FUTURE PRESIDENTS
by Rev. Dr. Charles Edward Mock

Robert P. Jones, CEO of the Public Religion Research Institute (PRRI), challenges us to grasp the profound political and cultural consequences of a new reality that America is no longer a majority white Christian nation. Jones argues in *The End of White Christian America* that "the visceral nature of today's most heated issues, the vociferous arguments around same-sex marriage and religious liberty, the rise of the Tea Party following the election of our first black president, and stark disagreements between black and white Americans over the fairness of the criminal justice system can only be understood against the backdrop of white Christians' anxieties as America's racial and religious topography shifts around them."

President Obama's legacy of domestic policy, foreign policy, and executive orders has been built on a distinctive foundation rooted in his unique, multifaceted personal identity and grounded in the fertile soil of global cultures.

His most famous achievement was his ability to balance his multifaceted character amid diametrically opposing ethnic and religious forces, not to mention political obstructionism. As a black man of African roots, he had to walk a tightrope that compelled sensitivity to Africa and Black America. Having a Caucasian mother means the president's tightrope included a Caucasian strand, which sensitized him to the humanity of Caucasians. This, despite America's historical institutional and structural racism built on an ideology of white supremacy.

The president's Muslim roots through his father made him conscientious of the humanity of Muslims, despite the small percentage who misrepresent classic Muslim humanitarian values. His tightrope includes a strand woven by almost two decades of worship and instruction under the racially-centered liberation theology of Rev. Dr. Jeremiah Wright of Trinity United Church of Christ: a theology that required a preference for Black Americans.

Out of diverse identities and values associated with each, President Obama was able to fashion a presidential identity that represented the best values and practices of American idealism—one that transcended race, ethnicity, religion, gender, nationality, culture, and creed. He advocated the values of his faith, honoring the Judeo-Christian values of historical white evangelicals but not at the expense of others. He refused to judge any faith by those who misrepresented and exploited honest interpretations of sacred texts.

Being a constitutional lawyer, he was able to accomplish a new, bold, visionary agenda, however, arguably, without violating the Constitution. He promoted and enforced laws and policies that favored no particular racial/ethnic group unless he could justifiably and justly do so to equal the playing field for those historically victimized by racism or marginalization.

Politically, placing principle over blind ideology, President Obama achieved what he has against incredible odds: more precisely, against political leaders who openly defied him, questioned his legitimacy as president, and openly stated that whatever he advocated would be dead on arrival.

What President Obama leaves behind is a template for future presidents on how to walk a multi-stranded tightrope without losing one's balance, dignity, and honor, not only as a president but as a devoted father and husband.

Rev. Dr. Charles Edward Mock is the pastor of Community Missionary Baptist Church in Erie, PA.

A LEGACY OF LEADERSHIP AND SERVICE
by Dr. Kenneth Clarke, Sr.

As President Obama was assuming office in 2008, the Christian Methodist Episcopal Church began to encourage its members to learn how to navigate the challenging times by adopting a philosophy to move from good to great. It was the desire of the Episcopal leadership to encourage its hundreds of thousands of members to become an "Essential Church" poised for twenty-first century ministry. President Obama's "Faith-Based" initiative, which focused on the economy, education, energy and environment, and health care propelled the CME Church to make a cataclysmic shift and to focus our energies on investing in people and in our communities. We made sure our members had access to Obamacare and adequate health care insurance.

Our great nation made a tremendous stride in the election of the first African-American president of the United States of America. The election of Barack H. Obama marked many things, but perhaps the most important of those things was that many, especially the youth of various races, were freed from the mental slavery of not believing, not knowing that every man, woman, child is of equal importance and can aspire and achieve. The election of Barack Obama served as a catalyst, but it was his actual administration over the next eight years that would bring an atmosphere of inclusiveness, whether African-American, Hispanic, White, Asian, Buddhist, Muslim, or Christian. While his election was a milestone, it has been his actual tenure and his years of service that modeled what it really means to be a citizen of the United States and to be unified in common goals and aspirations.

That's why our historic denomination, founded in 1870 by ex-slaves, shared the president's vision and urged its members to invest where we were and in each other. The church provided aid and outreach in Haiti, Africa, and other international places while investing in our local communities. In doing so, we demonstrated our commitment to becoming a changed people devoted to changing the world. The CME Church is proud to have stood with the Obama Administration during these eight years and shall cherish and honor his tremendous legacy of leadership and service. All of the denominations who are a part of the faith community know that it was God's "Amazing Grace," so memorably sung by the president at the funeral in Charleston, that allowed him to lead us for such a time as this. We all thank God!

Rev. Dr. Kenneth I. Clarke, Sr. is the Director of Cornell United Religious Work (CURW).

A FIAT OF GOD
by Dr. Charles E. Booth

The election of Barack Hussein Obama to the presidency of this nation in 2008 must not be seen through the narrow lens of symbolic reality. There are those who will simply define him as the first African-American president. While this is certainly true, one must not remain sedimentary with such a belief. This black man's election must be seen as a fiat of God, for he represents the hopes and dreams of a people who have been upon these shores for almost 400 years. On the night of his election, as tears fell from the eyes of the Rev. Jesse Jackson, my thought was that those tears represented the aspirations of generations long departed whose spirits hovered over that gathering and throughout this nation on that hallowed and now unforgettable night in Chicago.

Barack Hussein Obama came to the presidency with a name that was unmistakably non-Caucasian. It was as if God wanted to make it undeniably clear that a black man was about to occupy the highest office in our democratic republic. Mr. Obama became the living embodiment of his persistent and motivating slogan, "Yes, We Can!" Such a mantra now gives all of us, and particularly our young people, the driving incentive that noble goals can be achieved and long treasured dreams can come true.

Throughout the eight-year tenure of his presidency there has been the determination that, even against the rigidity of stubborn, political conservatism, right will still prevail and triumph over wrong. I am convinced that the written truth of history will one day record that with the election of Barack Hussein Obama, our nation, for one brief shining moment, manifested, in the words of Dr. Martin Luther King, Jr., the true meaning of its creed that "all men and women are created equal and are endowed by their Creator with certain inalienable rights."

With his presidency now about to conclude, the ugly scab of racism has been pulled off and that yet festering wound has once again been exposed. However, Mr. Obama's legacy is secure, and his eight years as our leader have revealed that he is not only brilliant, politically savvy, and calm under enormous pressure, but that he is one who has held firm to his convictions and the ideals that make one respected, revered, and worthy of emulation.

Dr. Charles E. Booth is the pastor of Mt. Olivet Baptist Church in Columbus, OH.

Mr. President

THE WHOLE RECORD
by Rev. Matthew L. Watley

My view of the historic presidency of Barack Obama is informed principally by my Christian faith and my African American identity. Like millions of others, I prayed for his candidacy, the success of his presidency, and, most of all, the safety of him and his family. It has been one of my life's joys to watch both his ascent to office and the excellence with which he and his family discharged their duties with dignity, acuity, and grace. Without question, the passage of the Affordable Care Act, his direct engineering of the recovery from the Great Recession, and the advancing of the protection of the American people from enemies foreign and domestic all benefitted indirectly but substantially the church and the black community. There are, however, two major areas that my love and support for the president will not allow me to overlook: his antipathy towards both the church and Historically Black Colleges and Universities.

Like millions of others, I believed that the president would keep faith with the church and the community that she has anchored since we have been on these shores. Not only was this hope proven to be in vain, but it was vanquished against the rocky reality of the many Obama administration policy positions and his own public statements that were explicitly hostile to the faith. The president was certainly within his rights as a person and a politician to "evolve" on gay marriage, or at least disclose his position if one were to believe his longtime advisor David Axelrod, who revealed that he always held an affirming view. In either case, what most disappointed me and millions like me was the lack of the president's trademark diplomacy, reasonableness, and fair-handedness in advancing his position.

The president presented his position on gay marriage as a matter of love versus hate. To suggest that holding to the biblical view of marriage is an act of hate is not only intellectually dishonest and not in keeping with his duty to protect religious freedom, but it mischaracterized the foundational gospel message, which is that God's love gave Jesus on the cross for all humanity to purchase our eternal forgiveness by paying our sin debt. For one who railed so eloquently and consistently against the "false choices" of many political debates, he failed to meet his own standard in both substance and style.

The other great failing of the Obama presidency relates to his hostile policies and critical statements toward Historically Black Colleges and Universities (HBCUs). His administration's changes to Pell grant rules virtually cut the legs from many of our institutions that were founded by slaves, share croppers, and the church. His critical and hardline statements toward HBCUs certainly emboldened their enemies at the state level where many of these schools receive their funding and governance. This sense of betrayal was stupefying for many of us who prior to his election would have argued against anyone who predicted that this would be the legacy of the first black president. Yet the record of the deleterious effect of some of his administration's policies, especially when compared to his Republican predecessor, is clear and unnerving.

Without question, the twin pillars of the African American community have been the church and the academy, which have consistently and continue to this very day to advance the cause of our people. In either case, he does not receive passing marks. Of course, his hugely successful, scandal-free, and transformational presidency should not be viewed solely through the lens of his record on the church and HBCUs. Yet it occurred to me that there would be more than enough pastors and leaders joyfully and rightfully lauding his presidency in lofty and transcendent terms, and so it seemed only right to acknowledge his whole record. In fact, this hero worship is even partly to blame as to why he may not have done better by our only two institutions. The widely held view that any African American critique of the president or his policies was anathema both because of our pride in him and the unprecedented hate that he faced bought the silence of many of our leaders at the price of the advancement of our cause. Because many did not hold him to the account, there is shared responsibility for his failures, even in the midst of celebrating his overall success.

Rev. Matthew Lawrence Watley serves as the Executive Minister of Reid Temple AME Church under the dynamic leadership of Rev. Dr. Lee P. Washington.

TAKE A LOOK IN THE HISTORIC MIRROR
by Wendell Anthony

One of the great legacies of the presidency of Barack Hussein Obama lies rooted in the perception of how black and brown youth can now see themselves. His presidency has been an eloquent metaphor of a unique grace. It has elevated generations of young people to see themselves not as second, third, or fourth class citizens, destined to remain entrenched in a position imposed by the world. It is no longer a hidden reality, which many have always known, but others can now proclaim, "I too can lead, govern, and inspire the world."

Our national and international image, forever inspired by this president, will live on both in the mindset and in the very spirit of our children for generations to come. The reality of having a black man, black First Lady, two black children, a black grandmother, and two black dogs living in the White House has left an indelible impression upon all of those who have been blessed to witness it. Our nation has been saved from falling completely into the economic abyss. Our stature in the world for many has changed from one of the ugly American to a dignified American. Therefore, the personal impact of this president cannot be reduced to just a footnote of history. When one considers the war of assaults waged against this president, beginning on the day of his inauguration through the end of his administration, it is a remarkable example of the grace of a mighty God. It must be very clear to all who would look that "for such a time as this" (Esther 4:14) Barack Obama was indeed the man for the hour. The great Persian philosopher Jalaluddin Rumi once said, "If you are irritated by every rub, how will your mirror be polished?" Our nation can be most grateful that this president was never so irritated that he failed to perform his duty, to remain steady, and to lead where others have never traveled. Unfortunately, it is a great loss to our nation and the world that so many opportunities for positive change, for lifting up all people, were not embraced but were rather rejected. Words from our past point the way towards our future: "It is certain, in any case, that ignorance, allied with power, is the most ferocious enemy that justice can have." (James Baldwin)

Despite our enemies and despite all political, social, and economic road blocks, this president fought to make "the crooked places straight and the rough places plain" (Isaiah 40:4). For that, we shall forever remain indebted to his administration. For those who may somehow fail to recognize the impact of this president upon the lives of our children, let me take you back to May 23, 2012 (*New York Times*). It was then that a five-year-old black boy by the name of Jacob Philadelphia, while visiting Mr.

Obama in the Oval Office, said to him, "I want to know if my hair is just like yours." The president lowered his head and said, "Why don't you touch it and see for yourself? Touch it, dude!" the president said. As Jacob touched the hair of Mr. Obama, the president asked, "So, what do you think?" Jacob answered, "Yes, it does feel the same."

Thank you, Mr. President, for it does feel the same. You may have been the first, but with God's grace and our work, you shall not be the last.

Rev. Dr. Wendell Anthony is Pastor at Fellowship Chapel in Detroit, Michigan.

A MAN OF VIRTUES

by Sister Jenna

Most recently, I have been asked to share my thoughts on President Obama and his administration. The question is one that deserves a proper answer and we must first start by defining what it means to be a true leader?

A true leader is one who leads with virtues, governs with love for humanity, has the vision that we are all in this together and wants what is best for the collective, as said by Dadi Janki a 101 year old yogi from whom I have learned about true leadership. This is where I have witnessed President Obama›s governance of America to be a perfect match to an ancient voice of wisdom.

As citizens, we have had the opportunity to experience what it is like to be led by a virtuous leader who puts humanity before monetary interests and values the importance of equality and human rights. This requires a unique type of virtues - ones that build, unite, and create positive changes.

President Obama is a self-made man with humble beginnings. He started leading from within and used his strengths as a community organizer to eventually become the President of a great nation. His Presidency is an example of what is possible when leaders model integrity, ethics, honesty, and virtues. From the very beginning of his role as President of the United States, the world came together as we watched his humble acceptance as he took the mantle to lead in a contentious time in America when people were seeking change. You see, virtues must be genuine, they are something from deep within the soul - something we acquire from God and use, if we truly listen.

Through his consistent and stable leadership, President Obama has pointed us towards a world that will work, and can work, if we continue to go it together. Real. No hidden agenda. Compassionate. Caring. And, he is not afraid to cry a tear when violence strikes at children such as Sandy Hook. He made it clear to the nation that he cares. A virtuous person cannot and will not hide their feelings of empathy. When God has gifted you with qualities, virtues and values and you use them, they are strengths, not weaknesses.

Throughout most of history, humanity has been governed by a survival of the fittest attitude. It has become so common to confuse manmade power for «strength» and virtues for «weaknesses» so leaders with virtues are not always recognized for such. True power lies in the ability to tolerate, forge ahead peacefully, breakdown walls without harming others, bringing people together and opening up walls of communication while at the same time staying true to your deepest principles that will last for generations and/or lifetimes to come.

During the Obama Administration the country has been led by a truly special human being who brought back the meaning of great parenthood, friendship, concern for community and the re-alization that ethical politics are possible, despite the challenges. Pure leadership shows character, uplifts others, brings benevo-lence, and unites us. Something is dawning on us - it's almost knocking on the door of our conscience, but maybe it›s too soon to recognize the enormous contributions of a man who stood by his values and virtues despite the challenges he faced on a daily basis. President Obama has given us a glimpse of what it means to have soul leadership and what is possible for others to follow. If you replay the many scenes, faces, conversations, moments of President Obama, and truly delve deep into what makes him so special, solid, stable, and natural, you just might discover, this was a president and a man of virtues who will be remembered in history for a much needed narrative in our country for the future in helping to find common ground and inner peace.

Sister Jenna, Brahma Kumaris of Washington, DC, Writer, Host, America Meditating

The Impact of Great Strength
by Dr. Vanessa R. Watson

May you be made strong with all the strength that comes from His glorious power, and may you be prepared to endure everything with patience, while joyfully giving thanks to the Father who has enabled you to share in the inheritance of the saints in the light. (Colossians 1:11-12 NRSV)

When I think of President Barack H. Obama, I think of a man who is a great leader and a great man of strength. The president of the United States is not an ordinary man. He is a man who is strong and remains strong and positive in the face of adversity and in the midst of sustained evil attacks. This earthly man has the strength only the Lord God could give a mortal man. President Obama possesses the kind of strength that could only come from the favor and glorious power of our Lord God.

On September 9, 2009, while President Obama was giving the State of the Union message before the joint session of the United States Congress, a Republican congressman interrupted and shouted, "You lie." The Democratic members of both the House and Senate sent jeers of disapproval for the blatant rudeness. Vice President Joe Biden shook his head while House Speaker Nancy Pelosi frowned. The boys and girls and the men and women across the nation and around the world watched President Obama with intensity to see his reaction. The president maintained his composure and stayed focused on the issue at hand. President Obama may have been upset by the rude remark, but with great strength he continued to deliver the State of the Union message to the people.

The incident taught children across the nation that you do not have to always react to name calling. It taught little boys and girls that you do not have to give power to negative energy, but you can maintain your positive energy so that others will hear your point without you stooping to the low tactics of others.

Thank you, President Barack Obama, for always taking the high road when others traveled the very low road. Thank you, President Obama, for not only being a great man and leader but also for setting the example of great leadership and always showing your God-given strength and your genuine love for the human race.

The second portion of the text states, "May you be prepared to endure everything with patience, while joyfully giving thanks . . ."

The leadership of the forty-fourth president paints the picture of a man who has endured with patience the daily intense scrutiny from a minority of the people in the U.S. He has endured with strength, dignity, and a sense of humor the attempted mutilation and laceration of every idea, policy, law, and decision that he made for the good of all the people. No matter what good he accomplished, there were those who desired to not only watch him fall but who moved to initiate his fall with a push.

President Obama is a politician, but there is something about him that allows him to keep the reality of life clear and to fight and champion for the undereducated, the underserved, the poor, the downtrodden, and the abused. His presidency has positively impacted the economy, health care, equal rights, human rights, education, and world peace.

As history and his story is written, President Obama will be remembered as an articulate, charismatic, sincere, personable, hopeful, intelligent, analytical, confident, and honest man. Thank you to not only a great leader, but a great man.

Rev. Dr. Vanessa R. Watson is an Associate Minister at the Metropolitan Baptist Church of Washington, DC and President of Empowerment for Success Ministries.

AMERICA'S LEADER
by Dr. Mildred Summerville

I wonder if, when little Barack Obama was born, he felt the pull of destiny to be something far greater than most people would ever dare to imagine. By all appearances, he seems to have had a relatively normal childhood, much like many of us have had with not so ideal family dynamics at play. Reared by a single mother and an absentee father, Barack Obama grew up to be a shining example of a man I'm proud to call my president. What was it that called to him to stand up center stage as a community activist in Chicago, an Illinois state senator, a United States senator, and then ultimately to ascend to the highest position in the land, the presidency? A career politician he is not. My president is a man who cares deeply for people, listens, empathizes, and seeks to improve their lives. Quite simply, he walks the walk and is an excellent example of what one committed person can do to affect positive change one step at a time. So if I seek an answer to my earlier question, it's that he was born to lead—chosen by the people for all people.

What are some of the qualities of a leader? I believe a leader is one who leads but is not afraid to follow; is decisive but inclusive of other ideas that benefit the overall goal; is encouraging, motivating, complimentary and shares the spotlight with his team as well as stands center stage when the daggers are thrown; is professional at all times, even when situations may call for another mode of operating. A leader is one who understands he cannot do it alone and seeks to bring together a strong team of individuals with skillsets equal to the task at hand. In my opinion, my president, Barack Obama embodies all of these qualities and more and has exemplified them throughout his eight-year tenure leading our great country. He's gifted with the ability to speak articulately to people across the globe, including dignitaries, heads of states, leaders of foreign countries, and, let's not forget, our most precious cargo, the little children. It's not uncommon to see him cuddling and cooing at a baby, reading aloud to a group of children on the White House lawn, or getting on the level of a little boy so he can touch his hair. Yes, my president is special and leads by example.

We know that a leader puts only the best people on his team. My president, Barack Obama, knows a great teammate when he sees one. He picked his mentor, the intelligent, articulate, beautiful, and loving Michelle as his wife, proving he is not intimidated by anyone who could help him to be a better person. Together Barack and Michelle Obama created two beautiful children, Sasha and Malia, whom they love unconditionally and seek to expose them as much as possible to a normal upbringing while serving as the First Family to the American people.

Consider that personal space and a normal need for privacy is hard to come by when everything you do is held up to scrutiny by the very people you seek to serve as the leader of the free world. To raise well-adjusted children in this environment is a feat in itself.

Over these last eight years, I've been proud to call Barack Obama my president. He's led this country with class and dignity in the face of situations and undercurrents that would have crippled lesser men. Yet in the face of all of it, he has emerged unshaken and ever vigilant, albeit a little grayer along the way. I've supported my president and will continue to do so. I trust the decisions he makes on our behalf, and I am confident that my president, Barack Obama, has my best interests at heart. Does he know me personally? No, but that doesn't matter, because he is a man of the people, all people. I certainly feel a kinship with him and the First Family, but it goes beyond us both being of African-American descent. I appreciate that the decisions he makes on my behalf are not made without a conscious understanding of how these decisions will affect us as a whole. President Barack Obama thinks beyond color, religion, or privilege. He thinks of what is right, moral, and just. I couldn't ask for a better leader for this country.

Dr. Mildred Summerville is CEO-Founder of Tall One Outreach Ministries.

FROM HOSANNA TO CRUCIFY - IT'S TIME TO REFOCUS
by Minister Leslie Malachi

And they brought the colt to Jesus and threw their cloaks on it, and he sat on it. And many spread their cloaks on the road, and others spread leafy branches that they had cut from the fields. And those who went before and those who followed were shouting, "Hosanna! Blessed is he who comes in the name of the Lord! Blessed is the coming kingdom of our father David! Hosanna in the highest." Mark 11:7-10 (ESV)

Dear Mr. President:

On election night in 2008 the Roper Center reported 95% of the African-American electorate voted for candidate Barack Obama to serve in this country's highest office and 4% for candidate John McCain. Over 5 million new voters participated in this historic election of the first African-American as president.

I still remember where I was, how I felt, what it meant to witness the triumphant entrance, the drive and subsequent walk down Pennsylvania Avenue on that very cold day of the inauguration of the First Family who looks like me (us)! I thought about those who had sacrificed and marched before, during, and after the '50s and '60s who voted for the first time. What a unified time, voice, "Hosanna" for some, of celebration we shared!

When the 2010 mid-term elections took place, state houses, governors' mansions, and Congress had different, more hostile faces toward the marginalized elected. With certain politicos planning on African-Americans not voting, Nonprofit VOTE reported that only 44% of eligible voters in our community went to the polls.

In 2012 Americans went back to the polls and 93% of the African-American electorate voted for your re-election as president, with 6% voting for Mitt Romney. For the first time in history the African-American vote surpassed that of all other racial groups. We did not just go to vote because a Black man (sorry) was on the ballot, but like all Americans we had concerns about national security, jobs, pay equity for women, the economy, and the social and political atmosphere that was and is what my mentor and founder of the African-American Ministers Leadership Council (AALMC), Reverend Tim McDonald, calls a season filled with "weapons of mass distraction."

While numbers were still forthcoming, exit polls noted 89% of the African-American voters voted Democrat with 12%, the highest since 1996, voting Republican. Many of those persons were sworn into the 115th Congress. But that night, for some reason, I could not help but hear "crucify him" by those with unrealistic expectations, those who were not at the dinner table, those who did not go to the polls to vote. At the start of what's called the "Lame Duck" session, you, Mr. President, once welcomed, once victorious, once with blessings abounding were betrayed. It came at the time you were preparing for the biggest fight—the cup that could not be passed—of your administration.

From "Hosanna" to "crucify," 2008 to present day, during your Administration we have experienced many things, including the rise of the corporate court, war on women, threat to democracy, attack on labor and collective bargaining, health care reform, government shut down, Hurricane Andrew, Sandy Hook, Trayvon Martin, Jordan Davis, Renisha McBride, Ebola, Michael Brown, Ferguson, "hoodies on, hands up," Eric Gardner, "I can't breathe," Emanuel 8, Orlando, Dallas, an obstructionist Congress, denied judicial appointments, and so much more.

When you depart the White House for the last time as its residents—the house that First Lady Michelle Obama so eloquently reminded the country was built by slaves who look like us—your legacy will live on. Not because you are a Democrat, but because you believe in democracy. The most wonderful event that happened after the crucifixion was, as you know, the resurrection.

You have been a part of the resurrection of hope, the image of Black folk, and for that I thank you. Thank you for the audacity to seek, run, and win the highest office in this land! Thank you for enduring the time of persecution, prosecution, and punishment through personal attacks toward you and your beautiful family. Thank you for a well-fought battle, "good and faithful servant."

May the Lord bless you and keep you. May His light shine upon you!

Minister Leslie Watson Malachi serves as Director of African American Religious Affairs, People For the American Way.

THE MEANING OF PRESIDENT OBAMA'S HISTORIC JOURNEY
by Iman Talib Shareef

Reverend Dr. Martin Luther King, Jr. said, *"The ultimate measure of a man is not where he stands in moments of comfort and convenience, but where he stands at times of challenge and controversy."*

Certainly, this statement is relevant to our nation's first African-American president, Barack Obama. Upon entering office, he faced the challenges of inheriting leadership of the world's largest economy at the height of the global financial crisis; a failed auto industry desperately in need of a bailout; the country's lack of universal healthcare after several failed attempts by previous presidents; significantly high unemployment rates; the nation being in the midst of an unprecedented lingering war; and much more. On top of all that, being the first African-American president in a society where his race was enslaved, degraded, and denied their humanity, he had to endure immediate racism from not just the white supremacist advocates in our nation but from those in the U.S. Congress, who swore from day one to block his initiatives. And it wasn't because his initiatives weren't in the best interests of and beneficial to our nation, but rather because of his race. His mother was white and his father black. He is a Christian with a Muslim and Jewish name.

Despite all of the above challenges, he was able to achieve hundreds of key, significant, historic accomplishments. And he did it in accord with the highest aspirations upon which our nation was founded. Certainly, as an American, a descendant of enslaved Africans, and a Muslim, I want to note in this reflection that his focus on the foundational values in the life that brought the pioneers to America in search of democracy and religious freedom was profound and reveal aspirations and ideals that all Americans (no matter their race, religion, ethnicity, etc.) can accept, identify with, and share with other Americans.

President Obama stood in the light of our founding documents, which are rooted in the fact that from the very beginning there was the fight for religious freedom, followed by the fight for all the other freedoms. Obama's presidency underscores that many among the Founding Fathers of this great nation and those connected with their struggle for independence and freedom of religious expression were guided by universal aspirations to establish spiritual life as the life for the betterment of society so that society could exist, have a good future, and progress in the matter ordained for it by the Creator.

This idea of the Creator is highlighted in the language of the Founding Fathers: *"We hold these truths to be self-evident, that all men are created equal and endowed by their Creator...."* Here in the language of the Founding Fathers, in this most important document, is the recognition of Almighty God as the Creator and a recognition of all men as having inalienable rights that the government can't give to them and that should not be violated or denied. They acknowledged that all were created with those rights. Here, we also find an identity for the citizens of America. And that identity, although expressed in masculine gender, is for females also. *"We hold these truths to be self-evident that all men are created equal."* There the Declaration of Independence recognizes sameness for all people and for all individuals.

Obama's presidency points to the fact that the Constitution of the United States does not base itself upon the identity or classification of a race or nationality. It bases itself upon the life needs and aspirations of the universal man, the common type, and the person that is in every one of us, the same with no differences. Obama's presidency represents our country's continuous steps towards fulfilling the promise of America.

In the language of the Founding Fathers was the building of an idea that would connect man to Almighty God; it would insist that government recognize it as a connection that government didn't make and cannot break. Essentially, they were forcing government to recognize that connection and to treat all citizens as *the creation* of Almighty God, *the Creator*. This idea, represented in Obama, is at the core of what makes America the beautiful. This idea of a government, a society that acknowledges that there is a Superior Authority other than man and that people are accountable to that authority, their Creator, who gave them their life, is what establishes a true democracy.

Obama's presidency is one of the biggest signs that we are witnessing a time of equal opportunity for all people in America. The days of second-class citizenship being supported by law are gone, as the law of the land essentially treats us all the same. Many American citizens have recognized these realities, this change, and have, as we should, embraced the good, the progress, and good purposes upon which this nation was founded. And it's wonderful how the spirit and language that the nation's founders left with us have gained support, so much so that we have progressed to elect our first African-American president. All presidents have said and will continue to say, "God bless America." Well, "Barack" means "blessed" in Arabic and Hebrew, a sign in him of one of the great blessings the Almighty has bestowed on our great nation.

Talib M. Shareef is President and Imam of the historic Nation's Mosque, Masjid Muhammad, located at 1519 Islamic Way (4th Street), NW, Washington, DC.

PRESIDENT OBAMA: A LEGACY OF ACHIEVEMENT FROM THE BEGINNING
by Rev. James D. Melton, Jr.

"It is fitting that with the very first bill I sign…we are upholding one of this nation's first principles: that we are all created equal and each deserve a chance to pursue our own version of happiness." – President Barack Obama, January 29, 2009

How amazing that the first piece of legislation signed into law by the first African-American president focused on equality for all citizens. The Lilly Ledbetter Fair Pay Act of 2009 demonstrated, I believe, President Obama's strong commitment to using the Office of the Presidency to advance equality and fairness across all segments of our society.

In only seven years, President Obama's administration has made advancements that reach every cross-section of our society. Sometimes I am asked by those in my community what President Obama has done for African-Americans. The Affordable Care Act (ACA) is great because of the number of individuals and families it has helped and continues to help; however, the ACA is not usually where I begin.

As awesome as President Obama has been by focusing on criminal justice reform, including having both Attorney General Holder and Attorney General Lynch very focused on changing systems for white, black, and brown Americans, I don't usually begin the conversation there either. I even have a family member being released in the next couple of weeks. This is, in part, due to President Obama commuting sentencing of a record number of inmates who were convicted and sentenced under unfair and discriminatory sentencing laws.

I don't begin with how, through President Obama's administration, the housing market was saved, the U.S. auto industry was spared, the unemployment rate has declined, and millions of jobs have been created. Each of these is great for the nation and the African-American community, but that is not my starting point.

Usually when asked, "What has the first African-American president done for the African-American community?", I start with The Lilly Ledbetter Fair Pay Act of 2009. This Act allows easier recourse for employees to challenge unfair pay practices. By signing this law, the foundation was laid. I believe what President Obama thought the Office of the President should reflect is promoting and championing fairness and equality across the land. Even the president's own words he spoke during the signing ceremony expressed this belief: "It is fitting that with this very first bill I sign—the Lilly Ledbetter Fair Pay Act—we are upholding one of this nation's first principles: that we are all created equal and each deserve a chance to pursue our own version of happiness."

For the African-American community, if we are given equal opportunity and chances to pursue our own version of happiness, there is no stopping us! Throughout his presidency, President Obama's signature legislations have helped very fragile segments within our society—the poor, unemployed, underemployed, marginalized, minorities, and women. Thank you, Mr. President, for creating an atmosphere that begins to equalize the playing field.

Rev. James D. Melton Jr. is the pastor of Stewart Memorial CME Church of Indianapolis, IN.

GRIEVING THE LOSS OF A STELLAR PRESIDENT
by Dr. Anthony L. Bennett

As I reflect on the presidency of Barack Hussein Obama in my "sanctified imagination," I imagine him singing the song by Brooks and Dunn, "You're Going to Miss Me When I'm Gone." Even if President Obama does not have that particular song on his mental play list, I believe that song is on repeat mode in the sound cloud of the minds of millions. For indeed the presidency of Barack Obama has not only been historic, consequential, and controversial, but it has left an indelible mark of transformative leadership in the heart of our nation's democracy. And given the incomprehensible vulgarity of the 2016 presidential election season, even noted conservative Republican operatives like David Frum speak of missing Obama.

My wife, Donna, and I have been in conversation with others about an indescribable feeling of sadness and concern when the Obamas leave the White House. It wasn't until recently that I realized that a part of the angst that I and many I've spoken with were experiencing centered on our hesitancy to acknowledge that we were actually grieving the conclusion of President Obama's term in office. While certainly we are not in any way speaking of the Obamas' physical death, I, my family, and the congregation I serve will join millions of others in coming to grips with what it means to live without a President Obama presence. I wrestle with this on many different levels: as a son of parents who were raised in Winona, Mississippi who knew firsthand the clutches of segregation and discrimination; as a spouse of a beautiful and critical thinking woman who, like me, has benefited from the outcomes of the Civil Rights Movement of those who came before us as well as engaged in race and equity movements from the '80s; as a father of a nine-year-old (a true Obama baby) and a twenty-seven-year-old whose life experience will include our shared reality of the first African-American president; and as a grandfather of a five-month-old girl for whom I am fearful of the world she must navigate. As a pastor of a predominantly African-American congregation, I am concerned about the state of our urban communities. And as I have shared with hundreds of families over my 25-year tenure of pastoring, I realize that the grief process is just that, a process.

I realize that the process often begins with numbness, in that we are in a state of shock. I am still sort of numb to the fact that I will soon awaken to a reality where I will not see a First Lady with the kind of brilliance and elegance that Michelle Obama exuded. I am coming to terms with the fact that President Obama had to, on a daily basis, stand with dignity and strength as God literally and metaphorically prepared a table before him and his family in the presence of their enemies.

Another phase of the process of my grief has involved bargaining between fantasy and reality. In my fantasy moments, I would join the dream of those who would like Obama to remain in the White House for a third term. My bargaining would include the ways in which I would have wanted President Obama to have fought more for African-American issues, such as an earlier public addressing of mass incarceration, gun violence, and criminal justice reform. Yet the reality is that there are term limits for the presidency. And in spite of my projections on the "green screen" of his presidency, he was one man who had eight years to do his best to lead this nation out of recession and racial strife and to re-establish relationships internationally. Which, in reality, is too tall a task for any one president to accomplish.

The third phase in the grieving process would be acceptance—to accept that some of my expectations were not based in a reality of American politics, especially as it relates to an African-American leader. To accept the reality that beyond the symbolism of his presidency as a milestone of African-American achievement, I need to accept his significant aspirational and pragmatic policy accomplishments on behalf of many Americans. In reality, if America is honest, this one man accomplished a great deal and overcame the cynicism and opposition that plagued his campaigns and two terms to advance this country's wellbeing nationally and globally.

The hope within my grief is to accept that President Obama did the best he could considering what he walked into in terms of the recession and political climate. As President Obama started his journey in public life as an organizer, I believe there is wisdom in a statement from one of the current leading organizers in Ferguson, Missouri. My friend and brother, Rev. Osagyefo Uhuru Sekou, shared, "Deference is not a sign of weakness or accommodation but rather an acknowledgement that the story of this struggle is bigger and older than us all." This statement grounds my acceptance of President Obama leaving office as well as the legacy he leaves behind. The Obama presidency is a stellar example of one man rising to the occasion to answer the call of our ancestors to transcend racism and bigotry to lead in the advancement of our struggle toward equality and justice as we demand that the United States of America fulfill her promise of true democracy.

For those of us who will be grieving the end of President Obama's term in office, whether we have critiqued his performance or not, we must give him the deferential respect of being the very embodiment of the tenacity, fortitude, dignity, intelligence, and perseverance of those whose shoulders we all stand on. Our ancestors have raised us to know that, in spite of the opposition and in the spirit of Dr. Maya Angelou, we will rise. Mr. President, we will surely miss you, but we know we must carry on.

Dr. Anthony Bennett is the pastor at Mount Aery Baptist Church in Bridgeport, CT.

Mr. President

A MODEL IN VIRTUE
by Dr. Delores Carpenter

The two campaigns, election, inauguration and eight-year leadership of Barack H. Obama as the 44th president of the United States of America breathed new life into the meaning of the word "hope." In the past, hope for African-Americans meant freedom, equality, and dignity. For all Americans, it meant the American dream realized in a nation where there is a level playing field and with hard work and perseverance anybody and everybody can lift themselves and their children to higher standards of living while giving back in service to others.

Despite the unfortunate negative criticism that always comes with success, Obama's contributions have been massive. He and his family have left the country better by far. Of course, Obamacare is a tremendous victory. Granted, there are problems with this huge system, but thousands of citizens have access to health care who desperately needed it. In time, it will work even better.

Despite the bipartisan operation of the United States Congress that had representatives and senators attempting to block Obama's progressive changes and improvements, Obama saved the auto industry in this country and turned around one of the worst economic disasters in recent U.S. history. He inherited a banking and mortgage nightmare; today many have recovered, though many still struggle. Job rates are up, and the president's approval rating is high for someone finishing two elected terms.

Liberation struggles around the world were encouraged by his initial election, and he has kept his word and brought thousands of young American soldiers home from war. In fact, he and his wife, Michelle Obama, have kept the spotlight on military families, humanizing and appreciating them both at home and abroad. He has taken an intelligent, technology-informed approach to world conflict and kept the country out of the chaos of the Middle East in ways that can only be characterized as brilliant. We have been proud of his performance as commander-in-chief, going shoulder to shoulder with other world leaders.

He has been one of the most eloquent presidents in my lifetime in terms of the substance and delivery of his messages to the world, to the nation, and to families and individuals about whom he has shown genuine and sincere care.

His tenure has not been riddled with scandal, nor has he lost his common touch. His humor and unruffled style have mystified his haters. Even when he received racial hatred, he came back with a smile and an appropriate comment that always de-escalated the matter. Long to be remembered are his tears when speaking about children being killed at school. He has called the nation to enact more effective gun control, all for the betterment of protecting the little ones.

He has been admired for his swagger. His use of the social media and television have been unparalleled. He has good taste in entertainment and has shared the fabulous White House performances on public television. In a way, we all felt a part of his journey. He and his family allowed us to look inside the fullness of his life to discover true role models for family life, as well as political life.

In Latin, the word "candidate" means "purity." We believed in President Obama and the credibility of his words and actions because of the virtue we sensed, and that sense made us feel safe. Unlike the political circus of Election 2016, we will miss this First Family.

Dr. Delores Carpenter serves as Professor of Religious Education at the Howard University School of Divinity in Washington, DC.

BARACK!

by Dr. Pauline Key

I've had conversations with a few of my friends who take exception to some of us calling him simply, "Barack"! He's the president of the United States, and their thought is that calling him "Barack" doesn't give him the respect he's due. They're wrong. In my eyes and the eyes of many of us across the globe, Barack Obama is more than just my president. He's a treasured friend, and though I may never have the chance to meet him in person, he will always feel like a bit of family to me. In his charismatic and genuine way, he has humanized the office of the presidency. The Obamas have invited us along on this fantastic journey they've been on for the last eight years. The White House will never be the same, and dare I say neither will I. I'm so grateful that in my lifetime I was privileged to be here while President Barack not only ran for office but won two consecutive elections and changed the face of our nation.

I am so very proud of this nation's first African-American president, not just for the way he's run his presidency but also for showing us the power of love, family, and tradition. These last eight years I've witnessed how our president seeks to give respect to people of all genders, religions, and races no matter their personal walks in life. Barack is the people's president, and he has led us with humanity, humility, and sacrifice. He's shown a spotlight on some of the places we weren't willing to enter, and he confidently walked ahead of us to start conversations we weren't comfortable having with one another. America is not easy. We're a melting pot of people as diverse as you can get. We were built on the merits of a democratic society where all of us have the potential to affect change. When Barack came on the scene with his message of "Yes, We Can," he believed it and made me believe it, too.

Barack wrote the blueprint on how to utilize grassroots initiatives like social media to galvanize us for a cause of change, which eventually won him the presidency. I would even go so far as to say that many will mirror what he has done because he helped raise the consciousness level of young people by meeting them where they were in using social media channels like Facebook and Twitter to communicate his message of hope and change. Young people felt included and consequently helped to take his message to the masses. Barack also cares about our most treasured jewels—our next generation. I can't help but smile when I see the countless images of children cooing under his intense grin, playing hide and seek in his office, dancing with both him and Mrs. Obama under the dome of the White House. Again, I say, there will never be another president like him.

Barack is a family man. He is present and accounted for. I find it refreshing to see how the leader of this country not only finds time to run the country but also makes it a point to exalt his wife with honor, respect, and love while living his life under the microscope of constant public scrutiny. Let's be honest in that black love is not often portrayed as what one would aspire to. Oftentimes the positive images and stories heard are few and far between. This is just one of the ways Barack and Michelle Obama have contributed to changing the story. Mrs. Obama, a respected woman in her own right, is a fitting partner in all aspects alongside her husband in rearing their girls Sasha and Malia to be independent, strong, and thoughtful individuals.

I respect his commitment and dedication, which started in his very own Chicago community and led him to the steps of the White House. Barack has cared about us for a very long time, and history will show him as one who wasn't afraid to get in the trenches to affect positive change for the betterment of the American people and to secure our future generations as we seek to align ourselves globally. As a Christian woman of faith, I see my president, Barack, as my brother in faith because his heart is for the people just as God would want. May God continue to bless you and your family, kind sir.

Dr. Pauline Key, CEO / Founder Pauline Key Ministries Inc.

THE LEGACY OF PRESIDENT BARACK H. OBAMA

by Bishop-Prophet Antoine M. Jasmine

President Barack Obama has revealed the true image of a great leader, role model, orator, author, father, and husband. In 2008, during the presidential campaign, we were won over by the slogan, "Change We Can Believe In," and eight years later we continue to believe and support the change. President Barack Obama is one of the most influential men of this century. His triumphant victory crossed arenas of power that no minority of any kind had ever experienced. President Obama has shaped a new culture of "hope" within the lives of many Americans and countries abroad. This is not because of the color of his skin, but because of the beliefs and values that he stands for. There is an old saying that "iron sharpens iron," and I believe the historical contributions of President Barack Obama have sharpened the edge for African-American men, women, and children across the world. When two iron blades rub together, the edges become sharper, making the knives more efficient in their task of cutting.

I believe the prayers of ministry leaders and parishioners have enabled President Obama to be more valuable as a leader. His presidential poise, leadership, and charisma have inspired many, including myself, to continually strive for excellence in our daily quest. His tenacity to make this country conducive for family, education, healthcare, and liberties has been challenged on every hand, but he has persevered through every test. The legacy that he leaves will impact the lives of many future generations. The progress that has been made during his presidential career can't be disputed and will forever be noted in the history books.

His determination shows that nothing is impossible and that hard work does pay off. President Obama's published literary works encourage us to become dreamers and to fulfill the purpose in our lives. In his first inaugural speech given in 2009, he said, "We don't quit. I don't quit. Let's seize this moment to start anew, to carry the dream forward, and to strengthen our union once more." The vision of President Obama has always been change, and this has been evident in every area of his presidency. President Obama has managed to achieve what many presidents ahead of him failed to achieve, and this was giving the American people change and a reason to believe in themselves, regardless of class, race, or even religion. President Obama has always stressed that when Americans do well, America does well. He will be missed as he exits into future endeavors.

It is my hope that the beliefs he stood for will continue to thrive as we welcome the next commander-in-chief. I salute President Obama for his nobility and achievements throughout his eight years as president. Thank you, Mr. Obama, for understanding that despite our differences we have a common bond—the pursuit of a better future. Your courage has inspired us to become revolutionaries and to stand for the change that we believe in. A leader comes in many forms. President Barack Obama exemplifies a combination of leadership techniques that show his versatility and compassion for the people he served. He is a great man of change who will forever represent the epitome of distinction, influence, and confidence.

Bishop Antoine Jasmine of Choice International Ministries of New Orleans, Louisiana

Mr. President

HONORING A GREAT PRESIDENT

by Apostle Rebecca Watkins

In President Barack Obama, our country was not only blessed with a capable and experienced leader, but we were in the hands of a true humanitarian and champion of diplomacy. He made history by being elected the first African-American president, but the mark he leaves on our country will be that of leading with heart. When I think about our president, an old adage comes to mind: "People do not care how much you know until they know how much you care." In these eight, hard-earned years, I never once doubted how much he cared about this country. We can only guess how difficult it is to be the president. No constituency is without its rough patches, but I feel as though he did his best to navigate the choppy political waters that come with the position. I do not believe I could ask more of any president than what we saw of President Obama. He poured his heart and soul into trying to change the system for the better. I felt proud to be led by someone so soundly connected to his faith. I felt safe in his care.

What I admire most about President Obama is his unrelenting effort to bring our country together. For countless years, we lived in a bipartisan country, and the spirit of this dividedness made us weaker. President Obama's dedication to making the spirit of our country WHOLE again is something that cannot be undone. He showed us that we can be bipartisan and still relate to each other as brothers, as sisters, as a family. We have never had a more family-oriented president. The values by which he led his immediate family certainly showed in the way he cared for Americans.

Barack Obama was courageous enough to dare to dream to change the world, and he did, in fact, succeed at doing so.

Because of President Obama, my nieces and nephews imagine possibilities that far exceed anything I could have fathomed at their ages. Because of President Obama, we live in a safer, more unified America. Because he bravely led by example, we can rest assured that the generation that was born into his legacy will rise to higher heights. In 1 Peter 2:13-17, the Bible says, "Submit yourselves for the Lord's sake to every human authority: whether to the emperor, as the supreme authority, or to governors, who are sent by him to punish those who do wrong and to commend those who do right. For it is God's will that by doing good you should silence the ignorant talk of foolish people. Live as free people, but do not use your freedom as a cover-up for evil; live as God's slaves. Show proper respect to everyone, love the family of believers, fear God, honor the emperor." I honor President Barack Obama and thank God for the privilege of living in a country that saw his presidency through two full terms. God bless him and God bless America.

Pastor Rebecca Watkins, AVOP Ministries

A CHAMPION OF INCLUSIVENESS AND EQUAL OPPORTUNITY
by Dr. Alice Ridgill

The legacy of the 44th president of the United States of America, Barack Obama, is a legacy filled with many amazing accomplishments. Certainly, sprinkled within the list of accomplishments are some devastating defeats. However, President Obama's accomplishments far outweigh his defeats. While he will be remembered for many distinct things by many different people, I will always remember Mr. Obama as a president who

Mr. President

displayed sincere compassion for humanity and who championed inclusiveness and equal opportunity for all people.

On January 29, 2009, nine days after taking office, President Obama signed into law the Lilly Ledbetter Fair Pay Act. The act allows for the 180-day statute of limitations for filing an equal-pay lawsuit with regards to pay discrimination to reset with each new paycheck affected by the discriminatory action. The Lilly Ledbetter Fair Pay Act, President Obama's first signed piece of legislation, set the tone for his equality agenda and was a huge step in the right direction for those seeking equal pay for equal work.

President Obama's devotion to equality is also evidenced in his nominations of two women, Sonia Sotomayor and Elena Kagan, to the Supreme Court. The confirmations of Sotomayor and Kagan marked the first time in American history that three women sat simultaneously on the Supreme Court. President Obama's nomination of Sotomayor also marked another American history first, as she became the first Hispanic justice to serve on the Supreme Court.

In an unprecedented show of genuine compassion and empathy for nonviolent offenders serving mandatory sentences, President Obama visited the El Reno Federal Correctional Institution in Oklahoma, making him the first sitting president to visit a federal prison. Some argue that his motives for the visit were strictly political. However, President Obama's actions during the visit tell a different story. Amid his conversation with six El Reno inmates serving mandatory time for drug offenses, President Obama transparently opened up about his own drug use as a young man. The honesty and transparency displayed by Mr. Obama point not to a president with political motives, but to a president with a heart for those marginalized by society.

As the first African-American president and first president born outside the continental United States, Barack Obama shattered many glass ceilings during his candidacy and time in office. His tireless efforts on behalf of the least and left-out of society cement his legacy as a president who worked tirelessly to improve the plight and condition of humanity both nationally and globally. His transparency, openness, and willingness to fight for equality and inclusiveness set him apart from many of his predecessors and highlight his enduring concern and compassion for all people. The bar has been set, not only for future African-American presidents but for future presidents of all races. There will never be another Barack Hussein Obama. Our country owes a debt of gratitude to our 44th president for eight years of selfless service and dedication to the citizens of the United States of America.

Dr. Alice Ridgill is founding pastor of New Faith Presbyterian Church (U.S.A.) in Greenwood, SC.

A MAJOR MISSED OPPORTUNITY
by Dr. Martha Simmons

The two-term presidency of Barack Hussein Obama denotes a watershed moment in American history. He forever jettisoned the neanderthalic notion that the White House was the domain of white patriarchy.

President Obama appointed 117 minority judges. He also nominated more than 70 African Americans to the federal judiciary, including at least 15 for seats on appellate courts. When President Obama arrived in office, 110 individuals had been appointed as justices to the Supreme Court of the United States. Two of those individuals were Black males. President Obama nominated the first Hispanic woman, who was confirmed—Sonia Sotomayor. He nominated the third white woman—Elena Kagan, who also was confirmed. Additionally, he nominated the 106th white man—Merrick Garland.

Sadly, in almost eight years, only four or five Black women made his short lists of Supreme Court nominees. He did appoint one of the women who made his short list—Loretta Lynch—as the nation's first African American female U.S. Attorney General.

I had skyscraper hopes that, if a majority of Americans could twice elect a Black man as the de facto leader of the free world, then surely he could nominate a Black woman to the Supreme Court. If not the man for whom Black women twice turned out highest among all racial groups to put in office, then who? If not a man wed to a regal Black woman with superior intellect, and the father of two Black girls, then who? If not at a time when the U.S. Treasury announced that a bandanna-wearing Black female freedom fighter will be emblazoned on the front of the twenty-dollar bill, then when?

What a major missed opportunity to provide little Black girls with a new view of hope and promise for their lives in America. Here are two, among undoubtedly many, reasons why I believe President Obama failed to nominate a Black woman to the Supreme Court. First, he feared the Senate Judiciary Committee would obstruct the nomination if he failed to nominate a Black woman who had a lengthy Federal Court of Appeals record—even if she was imminently qualified. He ignored the fact that there are many qualified, Black female law professors and jurists serving on the Federal District Courts, and even more serving on State Supreme Courts.

Second, Black women, although they were one of the primary reasons President Obama was given the opportunity to make appointments to the Supreme Court, simply were not important enough for him to place their names in nomination. Obama oversees the major political party notorious for erasing the indispensable contributions of Black women to that party. There is an insidious racialized gender erasure in Democratic politics, which "colors" Mr. Obama's normative gaze. The white male dominates the hagiography of American politics. Even with Michelle, Sasha, and Malia in full view, Obama's sociopolitical vision and the discursive whiteness in American systems disallow him to see Black women as viable political actors and the lifeline of his party.

Unfortunately, President Obama will never again have an opportunity to demonstrate to Black women and Black girls that the hope he espoused is broad enough to include their dreams and hopes. Maybe another American president, in the near term, will help Black women break the Supreme Court's glass ceiling.

Rev. Dr. Martha Simmons, in 2010, co-edited the 960-page anthology *Preaching with Sacred Fire: African American Sermons from 1750 to the Present* (W.W. Norton Publishers).

Mr. President

UPLIFTING ALL OF AMERICA AND THE WORLD
by Dr. James Kowalski

"When we recognize our interconnectedness and the fundamental dignity and equality of every human being, we help to build a world that is more accepting, secure, and free."

President Barack Obama

Thank you, Mr. President, for being a leader who understands that the greatness of this nation is best expressed through global citizenship. Thank you for the gratitude woven into every fiber of your being. It undergirds your capacity to see that things are not what they seem. You have been an example of citizenship with *sacramental vision* in your critical reasoning skills, your life-long learning with wonder and awe, and your respect for the dignity of all beings and creation. Whenever faced with polarization, the discrediting of science and facts, bullying and disrespect, you "went high." With delight and joy you reimagined and embraced our best selves and enduring values. In the great Traditions that have lightened the Darkness, you have been a beacon of hope to "keep us forever in the path, we pray."

The Very Reverend Dr. James A. Kowalski is Dean at The Cathedral Church of Saint John the Divine in New York City.

Mr. President

THE OBAMA LEGACY
by Dr. Joseph Darby

I had the pleasure of presenting a young senator and presidential candidate named Barack Obama at his first clergy breakfast campaign stop in Columbia, South Carolina. I still remember what I said—that the odds against his nomination and election were long and that his opponent had already wrapped up many of the state's African-American political operatives. But as a hymn of my faith tradition says, "God moves in a mysterious way."

The eight years of the Obama presidency are an affirmation of those lyrics. President Obama will go down in history as one of America's best presidents, not because of his skin color, but because of his service. His unprecedented rise from humble beginnings to the highest office in the land has made an indelible mark on our nation. A generation of elementary school students now finds it perfectly normal to have a black president because he's the only president they've known.

President Obama took the helm of a ship of state that was wracked by economic ruin; he righted the ship and leaves America economically strong and stable. He's made his mark on issues ranging from affordable health care to gender equity to a solid military, and has brought international respect back to the presidency.

He did all of that in the face of relentless and withering criticism and in spite of his political opponents' strategic decision to oppose anything that he proposed. His legacy epitomizes vision in the face of intransigence and victory in the face of adversity.

His presidency also, however, underscored the fact that America is not "post-racial." Resistance to change led to the rise of the Tea

Party and the election of a congressional majority that worked not to make progress, but to obstruct, and that brought many racists out of the closet and into the public square. His first term political need to be the "least threatening black man in America" was a source of frustration for some African-Americans who felt that their political agenda was neglected.

President Obama managed to rise above all of that and will leave office as a popular and widely respected president who has evolved in his second term into an outspoken advocate for the wellbeing of citizens of all colors.

The legacy of Barack Obama is strong and secure. Our challenge is to build upon that legacy. People of good will must continue to advocate for progress and equity and to elect politicians who embrace these ideals as they shape public policy. People of good will must relentlessly oppose and expose old racists in new garb who would turn back the clock of progress—those who blow subtly racist political "dog whistles" and those who now use blatantly racist political "megaphones."

When we stay on the case, we can build on Barack Obama's legacy, form a more perfect union with real liberty and justice for all, and do so in the spirit of the words of James Weldon Johnson: "Facing the rising sun of a new day begun, let us march on till victory is won."

The Reverend Joseph A. Darby is Presiding Elder at the Beaufort (SC) District of the African Methodist Episcopal Church.

Mr. President

AFTERWORD
by Darryl Sims

Here is pretty much everything you need to know about what this project has meant to me: My three godsons—Ricky Thompson, Steven Thompson, and Michael Thompson—came to understand the value of wearing shirts and ties. They all wanted suits that would enable them to acquire what they called "the Obama look." I could see in the eyes of Michael, in particular--the immense pride young men of color harbored for the man who served as this country's 44th president.

Nothing can measure what Barack Obama did to help young men gain a greater sense of their black male identity, dignity, and inherent self-worth. The president helped dismantle the pervasive stereotype of the black male. His undeniable brilliance affirmed the potential that resides within the brains of all young persons of color. He allowed the black community to be proud of who we are, providing at least a temporary reprieve from feeling like second-class citizens.

To be sure, he paid a price, one that included sacrificing the relationship with the pastor who'd nurtured him. He was disrespected by too many people from all ethnic, religious, and political backgrounds. But he remained calm and principled throughout. His administration was at once free from scandal and loaded with displays of compassion for "the least of these."

I express my gratitude to Barbara Williams Skinner and to the many who contributed to this venture. Mostly, I say, "Thank you, President Barack Hussein Obama."